MY KIT

Sybil T. Chapman

ARTHUR H. STOCKWELL LTD
Torrs Park, Ilfracombe, Devon, EX34 8BA
Established 1898
www.ahstockwell.co.uk

British Library Cataloguing-in-Publication Data.
A catalogue record for this book is available
from the British Library.

Arthur H. Stockwell Ltd bears no responsibility
for the accuracy of information recorded in this book.

By the same author:
Thoughts Along the Way

ISBN 978-0-7223-5072-0
Printed in Great Britain by
Arthur H. Stockwell Ltd
Torrs Park   Ilfracombe
Devon EX34 8BA

The author, just after she retired.

CHAPTER I

WAR BROKE OUT

When war broke out, I was six at the time and the three of us – Anne Pauline and Helen Letitia (named after Granny) and I – were walking home from Barnes Park, where we had been after Sunday school that afternoon. Suddenly, from a newly built brick bunker sort of structure with a huge 'horn' on top, there came a rising-and-falling scream: 'Eyhuh, eyhuh, eyhuh!' It was the first test of the air-raid siren.

We took off like the wind, me in the middle held up by my sisters! I think my feet hardly touched the ground all the way home to Homelands Park, where we lived.

Feeding the ducks and swans faded into insignificance. My family lived at Red Gables, 13 Homelands Park North, throughout the war and until I was thirteen and my two sisters had left home – one to university in Birmingham (Helen), the other to the Women's Royal Naval Service (WRNS).

My father was refused leave to join the armed forces as his work was in a 'reserved occupation' – supplying vital materials and components for the building of ships and aircraft.

During the next weeks, when many families were erecting corrugated domed shelters on their property, Dad, with all his contacts, constructed an air-raid shelter at the back of our house. The shelter proved time and time again to be our salvation. It had double brick walls, three feet deep, and a concrete roof with embedded railway rails. Inside were four smallish bunks, with power for a light and a small electric fire. The heavy iron door was opened using an iron spoked wheel – it was an old door from the lower deck of a ship, and it was encrusted with rust. We were living in a 'targeted area', particularly because of the industries of the Tyne and Wear area, so over the next few months the shelter was given good use and we had quite a bit of fun. Certainly we were more fortunate than families where the children were 'protected' by a dining-room table!

Life went on. Mum, born into a well-known family of artists, had trained at King Edward VII College, the art school of Durham University, and qualified just before marrying Dad. Mum had to put her career completely aside while caring for everyone else's needs, but she was persuaded to resume her wonderful work when it became possible in time to come.

We attended Sunderland High School for Girls.

My father during the war, determined to help, joined the police force! He would come home for a quick meal then go 'off to duty'. One night, when going to get the car out, a bomb created such a blast that he was lifted from behind the car, over it and out into the lane through the gates he had opened. Next door was severely damaged, but we were OK. When my father returned in the early morning, he was usually unrecognisable – covered in plaster, brick dust and often other people's blood. He was a very strong man and would stop at nothing if it meant *getting someone out* of a bombed building.

The first trousers I ever had Mum made me from an irreparable pair of Dad's uniform trousers. He painstakingly took them to pieces so she could reuse the material, and I wore them over my pyjamas when we went to our shelter bunks! They were much warmer than my Red Indian outfit! We slept peacefully and safely throughout all the onslaughts of the bombing, and the following day would be spent clearing up soot on the carpet from chimneys, or glass from smashed windows (despite the strips of tape across them).

In 1945 life resumed its path for us. There were great celebrations involving the whole community – sports days and fun days in our now peaceful park. VE day then VJ day were marked by competitions and 'matches' organised by the parents. I well remember winning an obstacle race where at one 'stop' I had to chew a cream cracker and at the next 'stop' I had to whistle a tune to that particular judge. The resulting mess covering him in crumbs! Oh, the *fun*!

I always loved animals, and during wartime when we had bombing raids the house got a huge amount of shock waves, resulting in the appearance of our first mice via the cellar then the kitchen fireplace. Dad dealt with them and introduced my first cat – Tigger. One day he was injured on the main road, and he managed to get into someone's garden. In those days there were only vets for farms, and the lady of that particular house called the police to ask them to remove him. I had seen Tigger in the garden on my way home for lunch and persuaded my mother to come with me on my way back to school, but Tigger was gone.

Other stray cats were brought in – usually stray cats from Dad's pub – but they eventually had to go, either because there was a mess on the carpet or because kittens were born. On one memorable occasion that happened in the laundry basket, under a bunk in the shelter near where logs for the fire were kept.

I remember Helen shouting, "Mummy, there are mice all over the cat in the log basket!"

They of course were very new and more-or-less-hairless kittens. As with others, it was my job to take them to the police station for humane dispatch.

We also often had dogs in a kennel outside, introduced by my beloved Grandpa, Mum's father. We had red setters and other large breeds.

Mr Bond, Mum's grocer, always asked her how the family were getting on during the war, and she explained I was by then "potty about horses", but lessons were financially out of the question.

"I have a horse which needs exercising," he replied. "Would Sybil like to take her on?"

Would I!

Once a week (in term time) I cycled to the field where Linda, a sixteen-and-a-half-hand grey mare was, seemingly, waiting for me! She came over from her shelter and nuzzled me, for it was love at first sight.

I'd saved and saved my pocket money to buy a hacking jacket.

Helen and me with Grandpa Campbell, outside
13 Homelands Park North.

My wonderful mother, 1956.

Dad and Mum at Wimbledon visiting Anne Pauline.

With Nancy (Mum).

My jodhpurs and boots were second-hand. Mum gave me a lovely yellow tie with horses' heads on it, and I had Grandpa's bowler hat (the riding fashion then). I was set to go!

Each week on Saturdays I cycled to Linda, groomed her and fitted her bridle and saddle. Then I led her to the wall by the gate, and via the wall arrived on her back. She was biddable and enjoyed walking and trotting around her field, with my voice of encouragement and – yes – love in her waiting ears. I trusted her and she trusted me. One day I decided to face the roads – and the tramlines – and take her home (about two miles) for Mum to see me in all my glory. She was so thrilled. And I sat one Friday evening for her art-society meeting as 'model of the day' in riding gear. Despite there being no horse at the meeting, I was so happy to sit still – for once!

Before school, we would search around for different-coloured pieces of shrapnel (still quite warm), and, like kids do with marbles, we would 'make swaps' with all the other boys and girls to add to our collections.

During term time many of the boys were at boarding school, but in the holidays we would get together, Dad giving lessons on how to correctly pass a rugby ball (he was a team player), how to best handle a cricket bat, etc.

The tarmac of the road around the park was kept in superb condition for our bikes and skates, and we played safely and contentedly throughout these years. I remember one boy's house had a huge multi-level back garden, where we contributed pieces of track (those lucky enough to have train sets) and made tunnels and straight runs (often damaging the garden somewhat) on which to time and race the railway engines. Oh, those were the days! Another had a huge cellar where we built model planes and ships from balsa wood.

Pauline was the first of us three to get a bike, so anything amiss at school regarding me was told at home before I got there. Some winters were so severe in the North-East we three sledged to school. Being the smallest, I was usually pulled up the hilly bits; coming home was all downhill. During winter the bike shed was full of sledges.

9

A Special Guide Camp (from Sunderland)

I belonged to the Girl Guides Association from the age of about nine years old, and we camped out whenever we could.

I was about twelve the year we went to a beautiful little village near Rothbury (I think) in Northumberland. Holy Stones got its name from its historical origins. Beside the Salmon Inn (is it still there?), where the postbox was set into its wall, there was a small gate which could only be passed through by asking the landlord of the inn for the key. Behind the inn was a large spring-fed pool with stone seats resembling toadstools and mushrooms. There, centuries before this, St Aidan – who I think travelled the same route as the Venerable Bede – would wait for travellers and baptise them with the waters of the pool (hence Holy Stones). Trees and bushes were all around, and I remember the gasps we gave when the innkeeper explained the origins of this calm and restful place to us. It was very, very peaceful and lovely.

The route of the Venerable Bede began, if I remember rightly, at Holy Island, which lies off the coast of Northumbria, and from there the Saint travelled to the mouth of the River Wear (the place is now called Monkwearmouth) before setting off into the wonderful countryside of the county. I may not have all the details right (it's about seventy-five years ago now), but I do remember the awe and attention with which we listened to this important part of Northumberland's history.

When Sunday arrived, we Guides all went to the church in the village – including, as usual, our standard-bearer. We seemed to wait for ages in the grounds of the church. Appropriately, the vicar was shared between three local parishes. Suddenly he arrived, wearing his black cassock and carrying a small case (for his surplice). To our joy and amazement he rode up to us on a beautiful chestnut horse! When he dismounted we were further impressed by his happy expression and humble explanation for being late.

"Who would like to give him a rub down?"

I jumped at the chance, of course, and was handed an obviously used length of towelling.

"That's all he needs," said the vicar as he went to prepare for the service.

Job completed, I remember fastening the horse to a nearby tree, and then we all trooped into church. What an experience!

I quote the words of Professor Noel Fitzpatrick at the end of a recent programme encouraging people to care more for animals – both domestic and wild.

"If you think you can't change the world, change the world for one animal and that's all the world you NEED!"

Likewise, teachers, if you can help a student to change their life – the rewards are quite immeasurable!

Helen on degree day.

CHAPTER II

FAMILY HOLIDAYS

With the help of old photos, I remember all the lovely family holidays we had. Garragill, in Northumberland, springs immediately to mind.

My father returned from early morning fishing in the river (South Tyne) and nearly scared us at the breakfast table with a gentle swipe of a large salmon. Another memory is of my mother 'losing me' one morning (perhaps I was evading her or Dad with another salmon?). She found me lying across the lap of a young mother in a nearby cottage while she stitched up a great tear in my dungarees! I was about seven years old!

On another occasion Mum asked the farmer whose cottages we were staying in if the large carthorse (which roamed around at will) would be happy if I were to have a ride on him.

"Oh yes" was the answer. "He's quite a strong and self-willed horse, but she's being riding around the fields already! She gets up via the wall."

When two angry turkeys seemed to be preparing to invade our cottage, I shouted for Mum as I backed away up the stairs. Her apron did the trick though!

I remember Dad with a yoke over his shoulders, a bucket suspended at each end, going to our well nearby for water. There was a stream which ran near the back door, but the water there, we were told, was not of drinking quality.

Low Newton-by-the-Sea, on the Northumberland coast, was another favourite spot. Sunshine, sand and sea – what more

Three of us by the waters of the South Tyne at Garragill, 1944.

When shall we three meet again? Skegness, 1952.

Guide camp. Me, front right; Helen, front left. Our captain agreed to my sister joining the camp.

could three sisters need? Not far away was Bamburgh Castle, which was a fun visit when we saw the huge display of Middle Ages armour and weapons. Further north of Garragill, of course, is Alnwick Castle, with its wonderful gardens, which I visited a few years ago. Dunstanburgh Castle ruins, to the south of our seaside cottage, brought even more local history to us.

Grandpa – Mum's father – had always arranged a summer break for his whole family at, I think, Embleton, to which my mother introduced us. It was so beautiful.

The beauty and variety to be found in the north-east of England, and the history that goes with it, would fill volumes.

Off the coast are islands where the early monks – the Venerable Bede amongst them – settled before travelling westwards so many centuries ago.

At Garragill we all swam in the river and I went shooting with Dad up on the moors. Mum, whose home as a child was a beautiful Jacobean period house in Whickham, County Durham, was able to pluck feathers, descale salmon, cope with rabbits, etc., and she kept our meals varied and true to traditions. My love of the open country stems from her. As a child, she milked the family's two cows, Daphne and Dilly, each morning before going to school!

Further down the coast lies Whitley Bay – quite a large town – on the outskirts of which lived Mum's sisters, Florence and Dorothy. Like Mum, Auntie Foffa (a childish version of her name) had three children – Atholl (following the tradition of Mum's family, the Campbells), Shirley and Heather. We went to see them sometimes at weekends after the war and I so enjoyed our games on the beach or in the shelter provided by the wonderful sand dunes if it got too windy.

Always Mum had painting equipment wherever we went, and many memories are revived when I look at her paintings around my house all these days since she died in 1988.

One beautiful memorable visit to Auntie Foffa's, their beautiful golden retriever (Juno) had her puppies on the large bed I shared with my cousin Shirley!

CHAPTER III

CHESHIRE

Suddenly there was a great upheaval. Due to Dad's work we were to move to Cheshire! Helen had gone on to university in Birmingham to study for her degree in English and French, and Anne Pauline was now in the WRNS. Farewell to the high school, where by now I had covered at least a year of the two-year School Certificate course (now called GCSE), and farewell to friends who lived around us and whom we would meet in the park. Dad had found a nice house for us with quite a big garden, and he'd also secured a place for me at Sale County Grammar School. There was a similar boys' school not far away, which we joined up with for choral events.

The new school came as a great shock when I arrived there accompanied by Joyce, who lived opposite to us. We went on our bikes – by now I had a bike of my own. What a shock that first day there was! Sale came under the jurisdiction of Northern Universities, as against Durham University in the North-East region. Not only was the whole curriculum different, but there were subjects we hadn't covered at all at the high school – namely physics and chemistry in particular. Subjects such as literature, poetry and history covered different periods, using different books. Somehow I got on with it – somehow!

At Sunderland High School we'd had a wonderful biology teacher – Mrs Collins, if I remember rightly – and at Sale I was able to opt for 'general science', which included all three sciences (biology, chemistry and physics). Chemistry and physics were completely new to me, and I struggled quite a bit. However, at the end of the first year at Sale, with the help of biology I was able to attain a credit in general science by answering, as we had to, one question from each of the three and then three more of choice, and my one physics, one chemistry and four biology did the trick for me. I have Mrs Collins to thank for that one!

A teacher and a carer, whenever Mrs Collins returned from a weekend at home in Wales she brought back for her pupils copious jars of honey to share around. At a time of strict rationing it had seemed to us like liquid gold! I do believe she passed that caring attitude on as an example to me in my career.

Anyway, with English, art, literature, poetry, geography, history and a reputation for sport, I achieved enough credits to get into college. Ultimately, however, Mr Bond's horse was also to help me at this stage, when I had to chatter on about a subject dear to me in my French oral exam. I remembered enough French to bring Linda (my pale-grey four-footed friend) to the fore. Thank you to my friendly companion.

I was now in the hockey team and growing up rapidly in the lower sixth form and studying as hard as I could in the first year of the two-year A-level course, playing hockey and acquiring (twice) a broken nose!

In Sunderland I had used every spare moment to work on Moorhead's Farm – it was up the lane, over a fence and across a field. There I learnt to call the cows in for milking (by hand), and many's the time when my head, buried in a cow's flank, had a halo of flies around it. One day another worker, seeing my plight, passed me his pipe to smoke – it worked, but my jaws couldn't hold it. Hence my first cigarette! Just about every day I managed my shift at the farm.

Sometimes the drayman went to Vaux's Brewery to collect the 'crowdy' (barley residue from beer making) and handed me the reins for both shire horses. On the way back the crowdy was still steaming and I was usually driving, aged ten.

The experience of Girl Guides summer camps and school sixth-form camps (usually involving helping on farms as most of the men had yet to return home) stood me in good stead.

So often, the farmer would look us all over and point – "You [to me], here's a key for the tractor!"

Oh, the fun!

My job was usually to drive a flatbed up to the fields to take, and then bring back, the workers, and in between to bring back the results of their labour – either peas or potatoes. We worked hard and played harder.

I remember one school camp near to a prisoner-of-war camp when a Latvian POW was with us and taught me how to do a double backwards somersault on the top of a huge haystack. Happy, healthy days!

On another note, the last ride for my friends and collaborators was most memorable. The farmer had told me to go past the gate and up to a gap in the hedge which the pickers had reached.

Up the lane we went, but suddenly there were shouts and screeches: "Stop! You've passed it!"

School farm camp from Sale – in the yard with Averil,
parking the tractor and trailer.

I knew what I was doing: I was following instructions! How stupid can one be! I pulled up suddenly and – oh dear! – those two sitting with their legs dangling over the tailboard shot off! There was not only laughter – but cheers. Naughty, I admit, but those two adults were really sitting in a very silly place. You could say they were sitting ducks. All was forgiven, if not forgotten.

Our camp packed up the following day at the end of our working holiday. A fantastic ten days! The school matron, Helen Lowenstein, had supervised all the comforts – campfire cooking, trenching around our bell tents after a day of heavy rain on one occasion – and looked after our general welfare.

A regular optional trip for sixth-formers was by train one evening each week to hear the Hallé Orchestra, and afterwards to meet with some of the musicians at a coffee shop in St Peter's Square. Season tickets were shared amongst us by our excellent music teacher, Miss Ruby Matthews. She also produced a good choir out of us, which sometimes joined with the choir of the boys' grammar school. When our school joined with the boys' school choir for a concert – I think celebrating the Festival of Britain (1951) – I remember singing my favourite songs – Elgar's 'The Snow' and '*Non Nobis Domine*'. I still remember the words! Ruby Matthews really opened up music for many of us, and extended our education by leading a group of us around the panorama of Llangollen, where her parents lived – an unforgettable day. You're still remembered, Miss Matthews.

I was well supplied with white shirts, which I was sent by my WRNS sister. On the last day of school I was persuaded by my friends, as I had no autograph album, to send my shirt collar (uniform shirts had separate collars) into the staffroom for all their autographs – I'd forgotten I'd be on the platform with the choir.

18

CHAPTER IV

CHOOSING A COLLEGE, AND OTHER PROBLEMS

The last two years at Sale County Grammar School, the motto of which was '*Cum sale mores*' (Character with salt), saw me growing up. Boys appeared on the horizon and thoughts of the future were considered. The sixth-formers were housed in a large house on the estate where the school was built. We had the advantage of using the old kitchen as a cloakroom, where there was always (in winter) a fire glowing. Also we used an attic room as a 'den'.

Cycling to and from school with friends (including boys from other schools, such as Manchester Grammar School), we soon got 'sorted out' at a corner shop. There we would sweeten the school day with meringues or chocolate eclairs.

I was very attracted (as were others) to a tall dark-haired handsome boy from Manchester Grammar School – a well-known and popular school. We became friendly enough for him to meet me at the end of the school drive and take me, on pillion, home via a lane where we sometimes paused for a quick forbidden cigarette! On one very difficult occasion I spent the whole trip balancing a newly made (in cookery class) lemon meringue pie in one hand.

When we arrived home my mother was always very welcoming, and she and he would discuss art, seriously, for quite a while. So much so that on one occasion I picked up his keys and helped myself to a trip around the block! Chaos reigned when I got back!

I remember my first ballgown when Ken's school celebrated the end of the school year and the advance towards college or

19

Me.

Kenneth Samuel Williamson.

university or other occupations with a ball. Ken's future lay (at that time, anyway) in medicine, and he'd been accepted for medical school. He also had a gift for classical music – I can see to this day his long tapered fingers – ideal for a violinist if he ever had time or opportunity. Teenage love grew and I was invited to accompany him to this final night of grammar school. My mother excelled herself and created a beautiful gown in pale-blue watered taffeta overlaid with a fine gauzy net in rich maroon. I had elbow gloves to match. It was a fantastic evening of real ballroom dancing with a buffet supper, then home – I was invited to stay the night at Ken's home. I must add here that his mother was a very sweet person, and she made sure I was comfortable, but nevertheless kept alert in case of any 'improprieties'.

When Ken and his parents invited me to partner him at a 'Christmas Dance and Supper' at his father's Masonic lodge I obviously accepted, and out came the same dress. For a sporty tomboy teenage girl this was the icing on the cake, and again I was asked to stay the night. We almost danced our feet off, and I was glad to be at rest without a further car journey.

With my mother and father both golfers, and he a club rugby player, then my elder sister, Anne Pauline, a trainee for the 1948 Olympics, it was no surprise that I chose PE and sport in education as a career with English and environmental studies, which also included the works of Plato and Socrates and their respective theories of education. It was expected in those days for a young teacher to be able to teach across a wide range of subjects.

I grew accustomed to the confusion of tramcars and life in a very busy city, and I was fortunate to make good friends along the way, but I cannot now – sadly – remember many names from my college days. We were housed in a prefab block, previously a military base. Delia helped me orientate in very different conditions from those I was used to. She was a year ahead of me and a 'non-resident' – i.e. she went home in the evenings and was at home for weekends. Very soon her lovely mother invited me to Sunday lunch with the family, and that became one of my very few absences from my coursework. It was an easy ride on two buses, but if it was very cold I had to be careful of going out at night. I recall riding back to college after an evening of singing round the piano and a few sherries!

Having been given, as requested, the course for the secondary age group (11–14 years) I enjoyed the greater part of the next three years, loving PE in all its forms from hockey to gymnastics, rounders, tennis, etc.

English lectures were good – even the theories about education as envisioned by Plato and Socrates. Creativity was the keyword, and art, music and method consumed me despite my second subject, which was environmental studies. College life was very good for me as I was so happy outside in the open or appearing in *Dido and Aeneas* as a sailor.

Teaching practice was a mixed blessing as we initially had no choice and were put where we could help. I had my first experience at a comprehensive school on the outskirts of Birmingham, and it was not very easy or happy, but was only for two weeks. I had to be well prepared and vetted by the tutors.

I also did a short stint at an Abbey Secondary School, where often chaos reigned. I was appalled by the 'prayer system' where the impatient teacher would call out a prayer interspersed with injunctions to "Close your eyes [name]", "Shut up [name]", etc. However, I got on well with those cowed children. One boy did play a really funny trick. He tied a long string to the handle of the coke shovel belonging to the stove which warmed the Abbey School pre-fab hut. I had to smile as the screeches of the shovel on the concrete floor were quite clearly heard. At the time I was endeavouring to show – with a football and an orange – the relationship of the Earth's globe to the sun!

However, this school was due for inspection and didn't want 'rookie' students around. My tutor arranged a move for me to Elliot Street School. What a difference! What a relief!

Everyone was welcoming at Elliot Street School. The headmaster used to pick me up near college and take me there, at the same time trying to wheedle out of me my day's detailed plans. It was wonderful there – the atmosphere, the cooperation, the interest not only of the staff but from the kids. The only really upsetting factor for me was discovering how so many boys and girls had folded-up newspapers under their shirts and inside their shoes!

These youngsters were really worth an effort. I was there for only one week, but later the next year when Final Teaching Practice came around my tutors realised I'd had a rough ride at Abbey School and I was given a choice. Of course I chose Elliot Street, where these eleven-year-olds and their teachers seemed to work with interest and harmony.

Intent on giving these students a wider experience, I set out to link music, words and pictures. My tutor OK'd the idea, but I'd never tried it before – I have since, though.

I set myself to help them enjoy Longfellow's 'Song of Hiawatha', linking it through Bruno Frost's paintings to Dvořák's New World Symphony. Highbrow? Hardly, the way I set about it. To get myself into the scheme, I was practising the largo from Dvořák's symphony on the grand piano, on the stage in our large college hall, little realising only a partition separated me from the college principal's apartment! I was well away in the old spiritual part when I realised I had an audience. Shock! Confusion! But I was greeted very warmly and left to it. The copy I had of the music had fantastic, wonderful, meaningful pictures to show while a recorded version was playing in the classroom. The children were entranced, and even noticed the political idea of the country of the Native Americans being overrun. Asked to try and learn a few lines of the poem itself, these children all chose the same passage about Hiawatha learning about the birds. . . . I could go on!

The last item in my plan was to ask them to show – on large sheets – how the young Hiawatha felt. There were daubs of red for anger, softer blue for sorrow and other splodges for other emotions. All the while the record was playing.

One day a tutor, as was usual, came to see how this student was getting on – the principal walked in! Arithmetic was 'happening' – actually simple interest – and I was asked if she might speak to my class!

"Do, please," I remember replying, but what came next was such a shock.

To the class: "It's good to make your money grow, but some

Delia and Grandma, Louth, 1952.

Sale County Grammar School for Girls, c.1950.

Delia and me on the steps outside our common room, 1952.

people don't use the post-office system. Can anyone tell me another way some people think they're keeping their money safe?"

"Please, Miss – behind a loose brick in the wall in the lavatory!" Totally honest and straight-faced!

The boy was commended for his facts, but he agreed that it was a 'bit of a doubtful place for safety or growth'!

On her way out, thanking me for my efforts, the principal's final comment to me (quietly) was "Aren't they loyal to their student?"

Bless those youngsters!

After my weeks at Elliot Street School came the leaving, and I was overwhelmed. One boy had woven, in craft, a red, white and blue cloth, which one of the girls had turned into a tea cosy – the previous year the Festival of Britain had taken place and everywhere had been bedecked in national colours.

The children had also contributed to a book their class teacher had found and shown them one lunchtime; and when I reappeared, there it was – leather-bound, gold-edged, the complete works of Longfellow. Possibly it was second-hand – who cares? It is a beautiful book, and I look through it to this day, sixty-six years plus later. It was the best experience ever of the short periods which led to my qualifying as a teacher. (Actually, Hiawatha raised his head again many years later.) I should also add that the testimonial I was given by the principal of Elliot Street School helped me along several roads in my career!

Delia with Shirley's dog, Hook Norton, 1954.

Out for the day with Delia, Shirley and dog, Hook Norton, 1954.

CHAPTER V

LEAVING COLLEGE

I returned to college for final tests, etc., and in the meantime the drama tutor – Miss Gibbs, herself a very helpful and energetic tutor/encourager – had had a tape recorder installed in one of the lecture rooms. People were encouraged to 'have a go'. Friends and families came to visit, and my four room-mates persuaded me to sing a song that they loved. We'd all seen the show *Paint Your Wagon*, and I'd also been with Helen to see it. I had enjoyed it. My four 'partners in crime' often asked me to sing one of the songs as we all settled down at night, and sometimes a thump on the door announced the presence of the tutor on duty! Anyway, on this occasion I did my best and my friends thought it OK.

Two days later, I was summoned to the study of – yes – Miss Gibbs, and, with a straight and direct look, was told, "Well, if by any mischance you fail to become a teacher, you could always earn a good living as a crooner!"

Then we both laughed. She had encouraged us to give it a go, and had been listening to all the oddities on the tape. Thank you, Miss Gibbs – at least you didn't remove my attempts from the tape, or, at least, not while I was in your room! Many times I have sung 'I Talk to the Trees' to myself, and it all comes flooding back.

So ended this period of college life.

During the half-term breaks Delia and I went to stay with her grandma in Louth, and during these visits I was able to complete, for environmental studies, my work on the development of settlement in Lincoln.

Staying with Delia's granny, Lincolnshire, c.1956.

Hubbards Hill.

Delia's mother, Louth, 1952.

Sometimes we visited my home in Cheshire, and Delia got to know my family. Her own mother was waiting for me to leave college so that Delia and I could share rooms together, and at that point she too could leave the family house – for very personal and serious reasons. She kept looking for accommodation for us, and at the second attempt she found just what we needed – space. We arranged that, until Delia left for Denmark to marry Peter, we would help each other through her second year and my first year as professional teachers.

Delia had already asked my father if he would be the man to give her away when she was married, from her grandma's house, and I was to be the bridesmaid. He was so pleased and proud to help.

I remember that well. I was at school's summer camp and I could get to Oxford for the hairdresser. (I wasn't then usually very caring over that part of my life.) Directly from Oxford, I took a train to Manchester, where Dad picked me up and took me home for the night. The following morning he drove us both to Louth for Delia's wedding, and for Dad to meet her mother.

Life restarted then, and I spent the rest of the summer holiday between Sale and my grandma's home in Macclesfield. To get there, I cycled over the Peak District. I got jobs on a farm, but could be 'on call' at night while my aunty, with whom Grandma lived, was on holiday in Belfast. My parents didn't know my future plans at that stage, but I had already applied to the city of Birmingham for a teaching post. In those days separate vacancies were not advertised, but one applied to the education department of the city of choice and teachers were appointed as needed.

Dad knew nothing of this until, one morning, a letter arrived for me from my headmistress-to-be – Miss M. M. Walshe. And what a lovely letter it was!

She said that as she was preparing the timetable for September, she would be very grateful if I would tell her what I *could* do and what I *couldn't* do; even what I'd like best to do and what I'd rather not do at all! She seemed so warm and caring and welcoming.

I had yet to have my twentieth birthday.

Enjoying the Devon Coast Country Club – c.1956.

CHAPTER VI

MY FIRST SCHOOL AS A TEACHER

So I arrived at Cotteridge Girls' School early to meet the woman who would turn me into a successful and – yes – happy teacher. All the staff greeted me in a very welcoming manner in the very small staffroom, which had an open fire! Small in number though we were, I felt all the staff had an empathy towards the children – 'The child comes before the subject' seemed to be their approach. That was fine with me, though nowadays I fear the attitude is reversed in many cases largely due to an overabundance of paperwork.

I gently opened the classroom door and stood looking at my new charges. Then suddenly Maureen – I think – stood up bravely to warn me that "Last term Mary ----- knocked Miss -----'s glasses off!" What a surprise for her! That teacher had lasted barely a year, but I knew her from college and wasn't altogether surprised.

My response? "Well now, but I'm not Miss -----."

They smiled (and so did I) then settled down for the register to be taken.

Then I appointed monitors for jobs such as giving out hymn books as they trooped out to morning assembly, distribution and collection of books for marking, blackboard cleaning between lessons, etc., etc., and there was no shortage of volunteers. There was even a 'flower monitor' – they already had flowers to welcome me.

Well, now we all settled in as per the timetable. I took gymnastics, with simple, basic equipment, for each and every class in turn, while my class would have maths, science, domestic science, etc., etc., Then I'd find myself back with my class for history, geography, English or art. Miss Walshe wanted hockey to be introduced, but as we only had marked-out areas for netball in the yard, we went to the nearby park. The ground was somewhat bumpy, but there was enough space to practise 'stick skills' and such. At least it got my class out into the open air and, in simple ways, introduced them to teamwork and manipulation of equipment. They loved it! Dancing – Scottish or widely international folk dancing – proved a really great hit with the girls, but perhaps not so for the surrounding classrooms! English was essential at a time when children's thoughts and feelings were not always given a free reign. They excelled themselves in story writing and other types of expression – for example, 'personification'. We made a collection of the best (voted for) creative writing then bound it simply into a small book. This is where craft in college came in very useful.

Ultimately, of course, the inroads of television and technology were to prove to rather deter creative thinking. I found later that these newer 'skills' killed off much of a child's spontaneity and imaginative thought.

A couple of the girls – Tina and June, I think – were given time in the autumn term, near Christmas, to work with their dance-school team. They usually took part in some great pantomime, but they quickly and happily caught up in January.

Miss Walshe encouraged me to attend frequent short courses, after school, to widen my horizons, though I had an endless collection of dance material from college. As secretary of the regional netball association (I believe) she was able to relieve me of netball-team coaching.

Home economics was a popular subject, and it seemed my class excelled. The domestic-science teacher said to me of Maureen, one of the girls, "You could eat off the floor in the big kitchen when that lass has been there."

One afternoon each week we walked down to Stirchley Swimming Baths, and from there the girls were dismissed to go home at the appropriate time. On one occasion, when I had to take a bus into the city after the swimming lesson, I asked Maureen if she'd take my kit home and bring it all in the next day. At that time I wasn't in a position (yet) to buy myself a sports bag.

The following morning, my maroon pleated college shorts had been sponged and pressed, my blouse washed and starched, my socks washed, pumps blancoed and the laces scrubbed! Now I understood the commendation of the domestic-science teacher.

I'd love to know if she took the advice I gave her after she had left school, when she found out where my digs were and visited me for advice.

Coming from an area where both history and geography were all around me, those lessons were interesting to all of us. I remember a lesson with wall charts I'd made of Norman architecture, and it was very useful later on when we went to Bockleton. In geography we constructed a wonderful, huge map – I told the girls to raid their home and grandparents' cupboards, and they brought in – so carefully – pieces of china, glass and porcelain. Then the towns and areas from which the pieces came were marked on the map – not just by name, but also with a copy of the glass or china's backstamp. A work of art!

Not all of my girls had first-class health. One lass suffered from bronchiectsis and I had to keep an eye on her levels of exhaustion, etc.

My college used this school for students' teaching practice, and, unknown to me at the time, our headmistress lent a visiting tutor a copy of current students' work – a copy of the class's creative writing. I didn't know this at the time, but, as one of his previous students, this work caught his attention. Eventually the book was returned to me – I still have it – with the praise of the college principal inside it! (And it's still useful.) It inspired me to repeat the idea of a 'class book' when I moved on to my next school.

By Christmas we were a well-knit unit, but I'd never have expected such joyous generosity from every member of the class. I actually needed two of the girls to come home (to my lodgings) with me, so many and varied were their gifts.

In the spring term, and still in my first year of teaching, something fantastic occurred. The city of Birmingham owned a large estate and house at Bockleton, near (I think) the Shropshire border. It's now, I believe, a centre for outside studies.

I was asked if I would be willing to take my entire class of thirty girls for three weeks' residential schooling and outdoor activities! Yes! Yes! Yes! What a chance! The idea was to take youngsters to get to know the world beyond Stirchley and Cotteridge – I could have jumped for joy.

These young girls had never seen a cow or a horse on the hoof, or climbed a tree even. They'd never been amongst wildlife (rabbits and such), and there were many gaps to be filled for them.

The day came. The coach arrived and some parents walked around to the school to see our departure. Luggage was loaded and I boarded the coach with a pile of towels in case we had any poorly bus passengers. This was long before the time of plastic bags! The light in the girls' eyes told the staff and parents all we needed to know! What views! What farms and animals we passed! What wide skies we saw! And they drank it all in!

On our arrival, we met Miss Poole, the very experienced teacher in charge, who greeted us very warmly. She was the boss. Then we met Robbie – known as Matron – who did all the cooking and most of the chores. She was a Geordie, and she and I hit it off straight away.

There was a Miss Boone, who was a supply maths teacher, and also Rosa, another qualified teacher, who organised trips to places of interest.

This was seventh heaven for my class and for me! The first thing we did was unpack then take a stroll around the immediate vicinity. My room was a separate room at the end of the dormitory. In strolling around, I pointed out the little church and told the girls when it was built, which many had actually worked out for themselves!

By now very hungry, we trooped in for lunch, leaving further exploration for later. The dining hall looked out over a large lawn to a forest of trees. Nearer to the house was a (climbable) fence. During the long and exciting journey there I'd heard lots of excited chattering, full of expectations and hopes, and I had wondered if they might be disappointed. I needn't have worried – the space all around was exactly what my girls needed!

Eager to record their first day – before breakfast, Bockleton Hall.

A cuddle for Nelson, Bockleton Hall.

Bockleton Hall.

Robbie and me at Bockleton Hall.

Keep fit on the lawn, Bockleton Hall.

Some of them made it up – Bockleton Hall.

Going back home – Birmingham here we come – from Bockleton Hall.

Lunch was lovely – healthy and plentiful, with Robbie's efforts in the kitchen paying dividends. I asked the girls to help with the clearing-up, and not one of them demurred!

I realised it had already become a little piece of heaven for them all. We walked quite a lot that afternoon, and all the while I was checking all the trees for 'safety'.

That evening we had another lovely meal, then after a short talk together they were ready for bed.

They loved their single beds, and I heard not one sound from the dormitory before quietly closing my own door. The facilities were excellent in what seemed to be a conference centre – plenty of toilets, showers, etc.

Next morning all the girls were up from bed on the gong being struck, and ready for breakfast. Initially I thought a few were missing, but on entering the dining hall I spotted them sitting on the fence with sketch pads. Great – they were using their own initiative and taking the opportunity to record their first morning's impressions. There were already one or two really promising artists amongst the class. Every morning thereafter we had lots of fun watching dozens of rabbits gambolling around each other on the huge lawn, with the occasional disappearance of one or two back into the burrows! A lovely start to a new day full of promise! This was before the deadly myxomatosis took hold. We had a very fixed but not too rigid programme for the following days – maths, English, simple botany, keep-fit on the front lawn between the trees, rounders and, of course, recognition of many new things.

I had a bare hour off duty each day, which was frequently interrupted by "Please – I've found a lovely tree – will you help me and show me how to climb it? PLEASE?" Usually it was Janet Bartlam who made the request.

Some afternoons the local vicar called in – twice during my hour off – and the girls organised a treat for him. The first time it was a demonstration of Scottish dancing (for which I had taken some records) and the next time was a poetry recital – but not as he or the staff expected. I came in just in time as they began to deliver W. H. Auden's 'Night Mail'. We had produced it as 'choral verse', all in a triangle shape, with 'dark' voices, 'light' voices and chorus

– I often wondered, later on, if they recognised it when it was used on the soundtrack of a television programme about the sad demise of that railway journey.

The vicar was stunned! So was I! Their perfect presentation – and without a practice run – was totally professional! I must admit I felt a glow of pride for my kids.

Rosa organised a trip one Saturday. I forget the town, but Woolworth's was the 'goal' of choice. Once inside, the girls were given strict instructions about where and when to meet together for the coach return. As it was a Saturday, lots and lots of people were coming in and going out, and my own memory of the exit is of feeling a hand pushing somewhat against my back and an elderly (female) voice urging me to "Keep a-buggerin' on, me love, and we'll soon be out!" Just to remember it makes me chuckle! I do wonder if any of my girls heard this little message.

We covered a lot of ground in the vicinity of the hall, and I thought I'd lost a few, so we backtracked to the old church and – yes – there they were, lying on their fronts making sketches of the lovely old Norman porch and doorway that we'd previously seen. Kathy Dutton and her friend Hazel were very active in art classes. I remember a superb picture Kathy painted, showing a train emerging from the mouth of a great tunnel – headlights blazing and a cloud of smoke all around, mixing with the fog of the open space. The class decided it should be framed – it was, and hung on the wall of the classroom.

Then came the day of the parents' arrival to see their daughters. After breakfast and a few moments of bunny watching they went to smarten up for this very important event. The arrival was to be – and turned out to be – a really special occasion. They tidied their dormitories ready for their sleeping arrangements to be seen and marvelled at, and to hear me applaud their total peace at night, as well as their general behaviour.

Suddenly a knock came on my door.

"Come in."

There was one of them pleading for a 'tidy-up'.

"Me mam and dad are coming," she said, at the same time showing me a pair of scissors in one hand and a brush in the other!

Soon there was quite a queue for my very amateur efforts!

The coach arrived, and they all rushed to greet their folks. What a commotion! The parents were really thrilled to see their daughters so obviously happy and healthy. They were allowed to show their parents around the house and grounds, and many a tree was pointed out with "I got ever so high in that one." Then, later: "Mind your step [on the lawn]. Lots and lots of bunnies are down them holes."

The parents were really happy about the whole set-up, and the staff organised a teatime break which they all enjoyed, taking advantage of Robbie's cake-making skills.

It had to happen – there were a few tears at the departure of their parents (all very contented parents). No traffic to worry about, lovely fresh air, and such a happy staff looking after their daughters!

I've often wondered if the girls still remember our time together at Bockleton.

After Delia left for Denmark, I couldn't afford to keep the rooms we shared at 39 Grove Avenue, and my brother-in-law came to help me move. My sister Helen (his wife) had qualified and was now a teacher of French in a school somewhere to the south-east of Birmingham.

My new lodgings were very near the county cricket ground at Edgbaston and only one bus ride each way to and from my school.

My landlord and his wife were Austrians, and they had been separated during the war – as were all those of German or Austrian origin. Their daughter, Lola, was at King's Norton Girls' Grammar School. My room of their very large house was on the second floor with very good window light, a gas fire and a kettle, plenty of space for my books and a large table to work at. There were three rooms on that floor, rented by Dr Yoshida (scientist at Birmingham University), myself and Masri, a Palestinian student at Matthew Boulton College – studying engineering. We got on passably well, though sometimes there was a queue for the bathroom! On the ground floor was Johnny Green – former Coldstream Guardsman and currently a builder. We all met for breakfast and some for an evening meal, with lunch at the weekends. I often had my meal at weekends – if I was in – in my room. There was also an Austrian ex-tailor, who kept us amused at times – Willi Flerishmann.

We all got along quite calmly considering all the differences in race, creed and occupation. At weekends, Johnny Green and I sometimes opted out – we went up to Clent and walked the hills, having a lunch at some pub, or we'd go as far as his brother's house and borrow a car to cover more ground and 'space'. Back at the house, we went our separate ways.

Apart from my usual teacher's work – planning, marking and preparing lessons, etc. – I also enjoyed a tapestry I had embarked on to give me some creative outlet. At times I would pick up my treble recorder, which had a very warm, mellow tone, and amuse myself. Sometimes I would answer a knock at my door as Masri wanted me to see his technical – *very* technical – drawings. Perhaps he thought I'd like to see them as I was a teacher, and he was very happy when because of my father being an engineer and an uncle being a naval architect I understood the purpose of his meticulous work.

Occasionally he would come in and say, "Please give me your needle so that I can sew [his sisters had taught him], and you can play your pipe for me."

It certainly had the tone of the Middle East, and my Jacobean embroidery perhaps calmed him. Occasionally I would notice an odd tear on his cheek, which he had to wipe away to see the sewing. He wrote copious lonely, sometimes hysterical and disturbing patriotic lines at this time, when there was much hate and disaster in his home region. This writing he asked me to translate into better English, but it was really difficult to break through his words, to fully understand them. As far as I know he had no other friends outside college, and I guess he ultimately went home and possibly died for his cause. He saw the folder of a college thesis on rock climbing that I had written and very carefully gave it a title: 'Path to the Clouds'. He also gave me, as a leaving gift, Book 1 of Winston Churchill's *History of the English-Speaking Peoples*. This was around 1956 (the time of the Suez Crisis).

During these weeks in these lodgings, I had the pleasure of

an occasional visit from an ex-pupil – I think to this day I can probably name at least thirty of the thirty-two girls in the class I had for two consecutive years – and very happy years they were.

Sometime during my second year at Cotteridge Girls' School, Miss Walshe told me she had been appointed headmistress of a new school, which had yet to be finished. It was in the lovely area of Bournville. Would I (and she also asked this of Joan) like to be the foundation of the new staff she was about to gather together? What a memorable moment that was for me! Of course I jumped at the wonderful opportunity. First, though, came my class's final weeks of school.

It was the custom then for a leavers' service to be arranged at Birmingham Cathedral for all those reaching their fourteenth birthday – some each term during their fourth year of secondary education – so I lost a few at Christmas, some at Easter and the remainder in July. Boys and girls who were leaving from all schools were taken to the cathedral with their class teacher by special coaches. For some it was a happy occasion; for others not so happy; and for the final group not happy at all. But they all supported each other, and the fellowship – for me – was a palpable experience. Except for one girl – Jose, who had only joined us for the summer term (due to moving house) – I had had the greatest pleasure of teaching these girls throughout my first two years of teaching, and I valued their company.

Sometime later, Jose Sola was one of the many who sought me out. She brought a huge bunch of chrysanthemums and was happy to see them immediately put in water in a vase of mine, on the table in my garret. We sorted out quite a few of her problems, and both enjoyed her visit.

CHAPTER VII

THE DAME ELIZABETH CADBURY SCHOOL

And so I moved onwards – to a brand-new school called the Dame Elizabeth Cadbury School. It was named after an important member of the Cadbury family, whose factory and grounds had been used and enjoyed – certainly by those living nearby – for many generations. The whole area is well known for its sympathetic layout. Cherry-blossom trees stand proudly on so many roads there, and a green-and-yellow mantle covers the village centre area, rich in daffodils and crocuses in spring.

The new school was for boys and girls, and a few girls transferred from Cotteridge to form a second-year class. Fittings and fixtures (for example in the science labs) were yet to be fitted – twice, actually, as different pieces of chemistry apparatus needed different shapes and sizes to be used! 'Square pegs in round holes' springs to mind.

The one class which transferred from Cotteridge was very useful in helping the new intake find their feet and giving them some idea that the three teachers already there were all 'OK'. We had no gym or canteen, so for a while the children would bring a packed lunch and the staff were invited to the junior school at the end of the road, whose headmaster was so helpful with lunches. His wife was our lovely, kind and very efficient school secretary, so the links were easily made, both by students and by staff.

My classroom was upstairs at the far end of the building, and there was a low-walled flat area through the back door of the classroom. When it was fine, we could stand outside and look

44

around, lords and ladies of all we surveyed. We could almost tell the time by the movement of cows on a hilly field opposite, beyond the park and the yachting pool. We could see the yachting pool clearly, and we would see the coming and going of the geese from Edgbaston Reservoir during the morning and late afternoon.

More and more teachers arrived to swell our numbers, and sometimes Derek (music) and I would go to a café for lunch and a little time to chat. However, the café was near enough to my previous school for a teacher who often annoyed me by turning up at odd moments to walk into the café with an "Oh, so *there* you are! I thought I might find you here." (Had I committed a crime?) This happened too often. Derek and I were good friends and supported each other while we found our feet in our new school.

Having left the RAF before teaching, Derek kept his pilot's licence and flew at Wolverhampton, I believe, two evenings a week. We developed a pattern so that we could get to know each other. Although my landlord wasn't happy about Derek's huge motorbike parked at the front of the house, we did at last have time to get to know each other on Wednesday and Friday nights. However, we ultimately decided we'd reached the parting of the ways. We became busier and busier as our work and the new building took up more and more of our time and attention. As time passed, district sports and athletics also took up more and more of my time.

Derek and I met years later at an inter-school dance session, where he was by then the headmaster. By then I too was in a different school. Happy memories!

From fairly early on, when I was at Cotteridge School, I allowed myself to be persuaded, by my class, to take the place of their retired youth-club leader at a hall in Stirchley. We had used hoops and dumbells for keep-fit, and with the help of Mrs Dutton (mother of Kathy in my class), who was an excellent pianist, we tackled folk dances from many countries and a little ballroom dancing. More and more friends joined, and socially it was a good training ground for the children in my care.

One year we had a long and prolonged freeze, and outside activities were not possible on the netball courts, so I decided to take PE classes in the park opposite. The yachting pool there was frozen over, and each morning the park keeper came over to report to Miss Walshe that the ice was thick enough to be safe. One lunchtime Derek and I returned from the café to find the whole school – including the headmistress – on the ice!

Nearly all the local families worked at Cadbury's – but those with other adults (grandmas, etc.) at home left their little ones and pre-schoolers in capable hands. Often my message went round to the class or classes concerned – 'Boots, hats, scarves and coats. Meet me at the school gate!' Across the road we would troop, and into the park. Then there'd be a race to get on the ice first. Sometimes one or two had spare skates, which they would bring. When we saw grandmas chatting, I'd pick two girls and take them to the elders to ask if their little ones would like to have a go on the pond with help from the girls. Yes! And Granny could sit and chat with a clear conscience!

I had already begun to collect some of my own poems/essays and so on, and after the first of many lessons on the ice I put together a small book called *Thoughts Along the Way* (privately published some years ago, and of which I keep a few to hand as gifts). One of the poems, written about the novel teaching of PE on the ice, is printed here.

CHILDREN IN THE PARK

The red disc dips and drops, as does the curtain of the night.
The glow fades fast and leaves its warmth,
A memory across the ice –
A memory of children, hurtling, sliding past.
A rush of wind, a body, feet, a swinging scarf,
Until at last she comes to rest
Against the wall, the edge, the refuge of the ice.
First one, then two, jumble and slither,
Knowing not where, just hither and hither;
Their voices break the silence of the air,
Their laughing faces radiant as they
Swoop and slide across this wide expanse.

They seem to take to flight like birds –
Ignorant of their gestures and their grace
They mimic gulls and geese, and race
Each other in a whirl of childish happiness.
And then the dusk, the herald of the night –
The sun drops down and swiftly goes the light
Of day, of hope, of happiness,
But they shall search and find this happiness once more,
This freedom and this joy.

Another poem was shaped while waiting for a number-27 bus to take me, after school, up to King's Heath. I was so so engrossed that I almost missed the bus when it arrived. This little poem was really an effort to put my thoughts on paper and, while looking across the road to the by now unfrozen yachting pool, to refresh my memory in years to come.

BOURNVILLE TO EDGBASTON

Twelve against the setting sun,
Stark silhouette of ash
Against a frosty roof.
The whirr of beating wings,
The honk of homing cries –
A fan, a vee, it matters not –
The rhythm's just the same;
Martial-like, and formed in ranks,
Gliding on and on neath banks
Of sunset-russet skies.

Whither bound, O geese high-flying?
To the kingdom of the dying
Dying sun across the lakes?
To the water, and the shallows
Where the 'fishers and the mallows
Hide among the brakes.
There to rest till dawn awaking,

47

There to lie till light is breaking
On the new-blown flakes.

Softer now, and fainter-sounding,
Merging with the dark abounding
Clouds of closing night.
Ever onward, ever onward –
Till no more on blurred horizon –
Till in memory only, fly these
Heralds of the night.

We had a very orderly timetable at the school, and once again I found myself teaching English. Apart from other sports, we introduced hockey matches on a real pitch some ten minutes' walk up the road on Cadbury's own sports field. I always joined in (even then, few could outrace me) and coached on the move until one memorable day when we realised a very high-flying object wasn't the ball – it was the head of my hockey stick! Great laughter!

I volunteered to take an adult evening class in trampolining – great for fitness. Although it was a poor sum, I was paid to do it. Then the ladies in the class asked if I would teach them formal dancing – ballroom and Latin American – and even brought some records in to help. Then we rumba'd and waltzed all over the gym. On these evenings, I didn't go home after school, but made use of the staffroom kitchen – usually I had a fried lamb chop with peas and potatoes. It gave me the energy for my 7–9-p.m. session with the adults.

With regard to English, I set about creating and binding a collection of the most amazing stories written by boys and girls in my class. Although the staff were all specialists in their own subjects, we all also had responsibility for a single class – registration, parents' enquiries, etc., etc.

About 1958 I was asked to take a class of the church's Girls' Brigade. As with Girl Guides, there was ambition to attain more and more proficiency awards and badges.

I had moved lodgings to be nearer to the school and now lived very comfortably with Lieutenant Colonel Pratt-Johnson and his wife, who had an enormous Victorian house not far away, with an easy downhill cycle ride to the school. Their own family was scattered – also in the forces – and their granddaughter lived there with her grandparents. She attended a very good school in Edgbaston. The house was big enough for us all.

Having spent all their married life in the army – mostly in India, of which they spoke with deep feelings of joy and a love for its beauty – they now were sufficiently situated to have space for us all.

Although I can't recall the little girl's name, I believe it was Lucy. We were both on the third-floor landing, and she often popped in before bedtime to spend a little time learning to play my treble recorder!

They were fantastic hosts for me – nothing was too much trouble. We often had rice with our evening meal, and the rice water was saved in the 'wash house' in the yard so that Mrs Pratt-Johnson could starch her husband's shirts and I could do the same with my blouses. If ever I was away she reduced my rent; when they went away they insisted I had a friend to stay. They didn't charge for my friend, but gave us free rein in the larder.

"The house is far too big for you to be alone in," she would constantly say.

One evening at the church hall with the Girls' Brigade I was so very stupid as to try and move a piano out of the way. (I used recorded music and an old gramophone for dance lessons.) I forgot about the knotty old wood floor. Disaster! The piano (old and iron-framed) crashed down on top of my ankle. There was, fortunately, a church meeting in progress, so one committee member drove me to Selly Oak Hospital while another took my cycle home for me. My hosts, needless to say, were very concerned for me – particularly when I reached home having *insisted* someone gave me a lift from the hospital. In those days there was no X-ray facility after 6 p.m.! I was instructed to present myself the following morning after nine o'clock! First, though, I had to contact the school to let them know what had happened.

Coming towards me along the corridor, Lieutenant Colonel Pratt-Johnson heard me apologising for my absence and explaining that until I'd been to the hospital I couldn't guess how long I'd be away from school. He took the phone from me and in his military way assured the secretary that I'd be there as soon as some arrangement was made for me to be picked up! The secretary seemed rather chastened.

After I'd been strapped and plastered, I returned home to pack a day's supply for my needs into a rucksack and slide – yes, slide – down the bannisters from the second floor (which had been agony to reach upwards when returning from the hospital). I knew that there would be a day or two of downstairs working. Lieutenant Colonel and Mrs Pratt-Johnson found it hilarious to watch, and I enjoyed their warmth and concern for a few days, having all my meals with them until I got a lift to school.

Once there, life was difficult. The head of English took on the job of carrying me up to my classroom for registration, taking turns with another teacher to supervise my class in assembly. I supervised gym classes from the side, waving instructions with my sticks!

One lunchtime, bored with inactivity, Ted Kestle, our fantastic head of woodwork, commented that I looked very bored. How about a lift (literally) to the workshop? There he showed me the available equipment and let me try my first mortise-and-tenon joint! I got so intrigued that I enrolled in his weekly adult evening class. I had, when younger, spent quite a lot of time with Dad when he did repairs or 'fixing' around the house, and I was quite familiar with most of the tools, which I was now taught properly and safely to use. The first item I made was a lidded box (eight inches by four) for bits and pieces – trinkets, etc. – the first test for my mortise-and-tenon joints. The next job was a frame for the Jacobean tapestry I had had some help with while in my previous lodgings. Sadly, as a sturdy and lovely firescreen in chestnut and ash woods, I lent it to a colleague a few years later (by then in my third school) and it was never returned!

Then came lessons in laminating woods to create layers of different colours. Then I learnt to use the lathe – a great experience. Having joined three layers, the block was cut and shaped into an eight-sided solid. Then it was attached to the lathe and worked so that the upper half was domed. Carefully, with chisels, etc., I cut out a slot in the dome and found a cigarette lighter to fit the size and depth of the slot. I felted the base of the whole piece, and now it sits, very typical of the sixties, on my dining-room sideboard – a wonderful reminder of my newly acquired skills. I think Ted Kestle would enjoy (if only he were still here) seeing the shelves I built in the pantry, the garage and a friend's music room to stack her collection of books and sheets of music on, and all the fittings in a bathroom I did for her in her bungalow.

I left Lieutenant Colonel and Mrs Pratt-Johnson reluctantly. The view from my window was of their wonderful long, long garden with the spire of King's Norton Church in the distance. While I was out one day he took the top off the large worktable in my room and fixed it with stays and hinges so that the medieval scripting I was doing to record the class's English achievements could be done on a sloping angle. I was with one of our school teams at a match that day and didn't know anything about it until I came home. I still have both collections of children's work, and they have had some use by a friend who undertakes home teaching with a group of boys and girls who need a little specialist attention.

To this day I'm not scared of tackling any job around the house, and what happened a few years later led to my writing this book! My bookcase (eight feet long and two feet high) is one example. It is still in use.

Sometime later, when I was happily engaged at Dame Elizabeth Cadbury School, with nearly all my non-classroom time occupied with games and sports, extra coaching for teams and home and away matches, I had a visit from a lady from Birmingham's education committee. I was told that she was waiting in an office to speak to me.

Oh! What have I done? HELP!

I met her in this little room with no idea at all of the reason for her visit – Why me? etc. – I assumed that perhaps our headmistress was expected to keep the committee up to date with staffing, etc., etc., and so I dreaded that something was amiss.

In actual fact, she had come to see if I was willing or ready to move on!

A large newish mixed comprehensive school – known as Moseley Modern School – was about to lose its PE mistress! PE, games and some classroom time would be my work. The school also had its own field (on a gentle slope) and a considerable area marked out for netball, tennis, etc., as well. The teams played in the district league and sometimes (in athletics, etc.) reached even the all-England school sports. There was a slight problem, though: we had not been able at college to reach into the skills of track and field sports except at a very minor level. At Moseley, if things worked out, I would have full facilities, for which I would have to embark on a summer-school programme – sponsored, thankfully, by the educational committee, including modern educational dance (MED) as well.

I was now in my sixth year of teaching, and the committee was prepared to cover a summer-school programme for me to attend at Loughborough College of Physical Education. Apparently my references were good.

What an opportunity! The teacher friend who had so annoyed me, but who seemed really interested in the idea of summer school, enrolled for their 'minor games' course.

I can't remember what the accommodation was, but I do remember going sometimes to see major places of interest in the area.

For me, athletics loomed large and enticing. Every day, with one short break for lunch, I and about seven or eight others who, like me, were working towards promotion reported to Mr Stamatakis, at that time the number-two GB athletics coach.

What a joy – both in the lecture room and on the track, etc.! The first exploratory skills tests showed me that at full speed I had a seven-foot stride! Looking back, I suppose that was why in hockey I was usually out on the wing.

Lectures were so well presented. Copious pull-out drawings of the body in action were a great help for my own knowledge of how I worked. My interest in this subject had been encouraged by my mother when, in the bath and splashing everywhere, I used to ask her, "What's working here (or there)?" These first two specialists (Mr Stamatakis and my mother) laid a firm foundation for me,

Loughborough College.

At Loughborough College – old style.

Sat on a piece of Henry Moore's modern sculpture, Loughborough College.

Loughborough College track.

which was to stand me in good stead in a few years' time.

Mr Stamatakis (or Stammy, as we called him) was so brilliant at associating structure with strength and direction – for example, in javelin and discus throws.

We were there only for about ten days, but what an adventure it was in my own field of action! The necessary certificate opened the way for me to my new posting at Moseley Modern School, although I left the Dame Elizabeth Cadbury School with many regrets and so many happy and successful memories behind me – ice on the lake and the regiments of cherry-blossom trees being but two of them.

I had no idea at all that so many years later I would be returning to Dame Elizabeth Cadbury School during the celebration of their fiftieth anniversary to cut a purple ribbon across the platform – the only surviving member of the original staff.

I was also the proud recipient of a sturdy wooden stand big enough for three flower pots. It had been made by children at the school with the 'occasion' written into the wood, which was apparently from recycled desks. It looks good on the patio and is a memory of the day and a reminder of the years I spent there.

CHAPTER VIII

MOSELEY MODERN SCHOOL

Now came the challenge of another move – to work under the headship of Miss Cohen (later to become Mrs North). I met this head teacher on my first visit, having walked up quite a long drive to the main entrance. She was a large and somewhat intimidating lady, and she ruled with a firm hand. Her secretary, Mrs Shuttleworth, was the wife of the headmaster in a city primary school, and from the word go we became firm friends.

I was given a tour of the school and its facilities, and it seemed huge to me. There was a positive air of work wherever my guide took me. The gym was well equipped, with changing rooms above and a small closet-like room for me and my kit.

When term started (1958, I think) I met all the staff and was introduced to the class for which I was to be responsible – registration, letters from parents regarding attendance, etc. 4R was my class, which I would be taking for English; I would take all classes for PE and dance, and supervise other activities for all other girls' groups.

I needed a bit of settling-in. I remember Mrs O'Connor, who taught secretarial studies to the oldest group of girls, was a great help to me with my settling-in and general orientation.

We had three Mrs Smiths on the staff, and I mentally separated them by their subjects. There was Mrs Muriel Smith, needlework; and Mrs Smith, music, was a fantastic peripatetic pianist who came to my dance classes to provide accompaniment for the lessons. We communicated so well and I'll never forget her kindness. I met her daughter Gretl in inter-school matches and Mrs Smith, music, arrived for afternoon classes. As she was a fellow Geordie, she always addressed me as her 'canny bairn'. (I also have a north-eastern background – and sometimes the accent.) I never realised what an effort it was for her until she began to meet me in the hall, rather than taking all the stairs to the staffroom. In the summer of the second year with her, her daughter phoned me and I was dreadfully upset to learn that having had to wait such a long time for surgery, her mother – despite the success of the operation – didn't survive all her treatment. She hadn't come through. It was a very great loss to all of us. From then on I used records for my classes – but it wasn't the same! She had loved her work with me, and I'd never realised how poorly she really was.

The third Mrs Smith was the daughter of an eminent vicar in Jamaica (Mrs Mammy Smith), and she lived not too far from the school. Her responsibilities were really with the younger classes and her classroom was the 'pavilion' – way out across the huge sports field. Not a happy place to be if she wanted her customary coffee break while the children had a playtime mid morning! She was a very honest teacher and loved all the girls and boys in her care – hence the name Mammy Smith. She and her husband had two boys, both at George Dixon Grammar School! Her nickname was not in any way derisory – she was beautiful herself and looked after those in her care as she did her own children.

When Jamaica achieved independence she, with the help of a grant from the authorities, and roping in all our boys and girls of Nigerian or Jamaican heritage, laid on a magnificent tea for all the staff to celebrate the event.

What a joy to see them! Some had cooked, and all of them served that celebratory tea. Every child had dressed for the event – pretty dresses and sweet hair ribbons for the girls; properly tied ties and pressed shirts and shorts for the boys. We smiled all the time – not one sock to be adjusted or hair out of place! A joy to be seen!

It was a lovely gesture – an extension of the social welfare Mrs Smith gave to the community where she lived. Sadly, I heard a few months later that Mrs Smith had died, I have no doubt worn out by all her caring and sharing with and for others, and I still feel her working situation was a contributory factor. She was a great loss to the whole community.

When a timetable for a new term was rather delayed, the staff made their own arrangements for their classes. I continued to teach them English; another colleague would come in to teach them maths, etc., etc.

My own class was very lucky – our classroom opened on to a wide corridor, and opposite to us was one of three sets of double doors into the assembly hall. There I set up the gramophone, and they willingly changed shoes, etc., and we embarked on a simplified ballroom and Latin American dancing lesson. Well aware of others nearby, we kept the volume reasonably down. It was a hit from the first session onwards. The à la mode winkle-pickers were changed for more suitable footwear, and blazers were cast aside – tidily!

Many years later, shopping in Birmingham with a friend, I came face-to-face with a young lady who had been in many of the dance classes. She had married a Polish gentleman in Australia, and now she was showing him around her home city. I was puzzled, then suddenly remembered her dance skills in the paso doble, etc. Then, and only then, did I remember her name. They both seemed very, very happy – he to meet her family and she to show him her city and meet me.

The year she had left school, I had been given permission to organise an evening of dance for them all, and I think this particular girl (Bernadette) played a large part in the organisation. They charged each other and spent the cash on light refreshments and a little three-piece band for the interval. On my arrival, coming downstairs to meet me were two of my boys – one nicknamed Doug, the other Cag – and they each gave me a little china memento – a wee cat from Cag and a little dog from Doug.

At the end of the evening, as we were saying our farewells, a girl (I think Bernadette) came to me to give me a bag of cash!

"What's this for?"

"Well, you've worn out some of your records and now you can replace them!"

"What a lovely gesture! And yes, we all sang 'Auld Lang Syne'.

The headmistress – when I told her how lovely and how calm the whole event had been – demanded the takings.

"I'll put half in the school fund," I said, "and with the rest I will do what the youngsters want me to do in view of the efforts I've put in to teach them and – yes – wear out quite a few of my own records!"

Sometime during my third year at Moseley Modern School I was in urgent need of new ski boots and a competition had been published with ski equipment as the prize. Competitors had to fill in blanks on an advertisement for a particular area to win the prize! Many of the blank spaces required geographical or geological words or phrases.

A couple of friends on the staff helped me to fill in the gaps, and yes – I won the boots I needed. Even after my ski holiday (Easter holiday weeks) I was still being asked if I knew which phrase had done it for me!

The following year I needed a new ski sweater and cap, so again the staff (ladies this time) helped me. One knitted two sleeves, another the front, and another the back. Then I put all four pieces on a circular needle to do the patterned part up to the neck. The pattern was one I'd bought in Norway, and the Danish grandma of one of my girls had translated it for me! Dear Mrs Shuttleworth, our secretary, made the cap. All the Smiths were involved, and one of the men on the staff wondered, with all those needles going at lunchtime, if we were going to introduce a new school uniform!

Some years later, shopping in Moseley village, I was looking for some nice lamb chops. On entering the butcher's shop I was met by a tall and broad young man wearing a butcher's apron with a hatchet in one hand!

"Hello, Miss. Nice to see you. Can I help you?"

It was either Doug or Cag of recent history! We chatted and laughed for quite a while, then I went home with two beautiful (free) lamb chops. The warmth of some of these casual meetings with ex-students remains with me to this day.

A new term at Moseley Modern School began, and by now I had been able to persuade the headmistress that the girls needed a distinctive kit. Some of them were by now in teams playing in inter-school friendly matches, and some girls were going further into district competitions. I managed to do a deal with an excellent company in Sheffield. Beginning with the removal of earlier beach attire, the school acquired a very smart uniform outfit – red polo shirts, green wrap-around skirts (and pants beneath), green pullovers/sweatshirts, green tracksuits for open-air activities and, for some, black leotards for dance. Now when team photos were taken after many successful matches or larger competitions, every one of the girls was proud to represent the school. On one occasion, at a district rally, an inspector asked me to detain the girls while she fetched her camera from the car. She'd never seen Moseley Modern School girls so smart and successful!

By now I had a small car, so I could get around more easily.

1961 arrived, and with it yet again a representative from Birmingham's education committee, seemingly to lay the foundation for me to make another move. In this case it was to be a welcome promotion in every way. Yardley Grammar School was one of only four mixed grammar schools in Birmingham at that time, and (as with my previous move) it was about to lose its PE and games mistress.

This was a very big step. Should I? Shouldn't I? As previously happened, there was also a condition attached. Yet another subject was to be introduced – modern educational dance (MED). The move suddenly become an exciting prospect. I was well trained in true folk dancing, and music was a must for me in many ways; now the thought of experiencing this new addition to the arts was quite exciting, though I must admit it was also somewhat daunting in its – to me – intangibility.

I was to be seconded to Canley – the PE department of Warwick University – I was told. Also I would be expected to teach up to, if not beyond, eighteen-year-olds. That was no problem – I looked forward to the challenge. And there would be teaching practice to face – as in my first college.

The secondment was to be for a full year, and to my joy it

would also include lectures in anatomy and physiology delivered by a physiotherapist/lecturer, Mrs Young. It seemed yet another gift to me!

Unlike others in this group (there were ten or twelve of us), I didn't need to be a resident student. My home was a flat jointly rented with another teacher, and from there I could get to the college with a 6-a.m. start quite easily. I would return home sometimes as late as 11 p.m. Then there would be notes, etc., to bring up to date from the day well spent. One of us was from Cornwall, another from Manchester, and once or twice I'd bring two others home for a weekend break as the flat was very large.

The teacher and I had decided to share this flat in King's Norton, which was near enough for an easy run to our respective schools. Her mother had died and she didn't want to live with her father. Our rooms were large and airy and we had part of the huge garden with lots of apple and pear trees – I was able to keep the domestic-science department very well supplied for the making of jams and jellies, etc.! It was from there that I drove to and from Canley every working day.

An extra activity was introduced – lacrosse – and as a sprinter I enjoyed it very much, though the cradling of the stick took some practice!

The time for teaching practice approached, and because of my route I was sent to Tudor Grange Girls' School in Solihull, which I would normally pass twice each day. I'll admit the tutor concerned made it as easy as she could in respect of the travelling.

In 1960 I had been invited by a colleague in another school to be an 'extra adult' in a school trip she was organising to Oberammergau, followed by transfer to Rome for the Olympic Games.

It was a terrific undertaking. Her headmistress invited two of her friends – not as staff, but apparently as holidaymakers. There's a big difference!

Oberammergau Passion Play is performed every ten years and the players are nearly all local people. Participants all have to grow their hair to biblical dimensions, which caused a lot of surprises as we drove through the town to our hostel.

Moseley's girls' athletics team. Me, middle row, second from left, c.1958.

*With Mrs Smith (piano) outside the gym after a
dance performance at Moseley Modern School.*

In the evening we arrived, Marie (the leader of the trip) and I set off down the steep meadow to the theatre to test how long it would take to get the girls there – in particular one girl, so courageous and unselfconscious (or so she seemed) about her artificial leg. Following a road accident a few years previously, she had had to undergo serious surgery. The costs that she was awarded were at that time in the safety and jurisdiction of the court, but her parents applied to the court and sufficient funds were released to pay for this opportunity for her. We had to be seated by, I think, 8 a.m. There would be one interval to stretch one's legs, etc., then the play would resume for virtually the rest of the afternoon.

Oberammergau lies in a basin surrounded by mountaintops, and on one of them can be seen a cross, lit up at night.

Outside the theatre were tethered all the animals that the story includes, and it was lovely to be amongst them during the interval! Inside the theatre, all the audience is under good cover, but the whole stage area is open to the elements and, wherever you sit, you see the mountains and the cross. If it rains, it rains, and the play goes on.

I can't think of any one child aged probably from thirteen upwards who was not totally absorbed from start to finish.

We went back to the hostel for our evening meal (we had taken sandwiches with us for the day), and I can't say the girls were even tired – though they were very, very much emotionally affected after being wrapped around with that beautiful depiction of the historical and revered story that is at the heart of our Christian lives. The animals they met were quite a highlight for them!

The train journey to Rome could have been a total disaster as all our reserved seats had been usurped – mostly by people going to Rome (including three of our own number) – but in the corridor, leaning on the window rail, it was possible to nod off sitting with bent knees against the door of the carriage that should have been for us. Marie and I sometimes nodded off with a child leaning on both our shoulders, moving only if someone needed to go down the corridor.

We arrived at our accommodation; as usual in most countries that have to provide for a mass incoming of visitors, our beds were all in a large hall – possibly a school hall. The first day was spent watching a swimming event where one English girl was outstandingly successful. We always made time for a walkabout after sitting for some time at the event. Another day we had seats for track and field events. This was before strict rules against medical enhancements really took hold, and it was sad to find out afterwards that two sisters (not British) involved that day had had their 'successes' annulled. Nowadays it wouldn't happen – disqualification resulting in loss of status, etc.

One day we went to the seaside and it was so relaxing for all of us. I, of course, was expected to watch those who ventured into the water, particularly if they were out of their depth. Even our intrepid injured child bravely hopped the wavelets and laughed so happily.

The day after that we faced the long journey home – all intact. No one was poorly or suffering, and all were very very impressed by their many new experiences.

Early days of skiing in the Dolomites, 1973.

CHAPTER IX

AND SO TO CANLEY

One could say that I was almost being bribed in this next venture. The truth really is that I was thrilled to bits to be offered the chance to widen my interests and experiences and attain my dream. Even the college's staff's consideration of the fact that I would be driving both ways between King's Norton and Canley every day had been in my favour. A good school lay on the route, and there I had done the inevitable teaching practice before the course ended, having added another string to my bow by way of wider experiences. It was also a generous requirement of the education committee that I maintained my salary for that course – hence the term 'secondment'!

The year in the PE department of Warwick University's campus passed quite smoothly. Our dashes between various buildings (gym, hall, lecture rooms, etc.) were somewhat frantic at times as we had to run the gauntlet of builders, carpenters and piles of building materials while wearing leotards and little else! Hence the need for our big black cloaks.

I had often wondered how I would get on if offered a chance to play the game of lacrosse, until one of the tutors (herself an ex-England player, I'm sure) introduced us to it!

As far as I can remember, we flailed around with our crosses like a horde of invading Norsemen and had a lot of fun. Handling the crosse and catching the ball, or throwing it out in various directions, takes a lot of skill, as does cradling the ball on the run.

For me, as an athlete, the running was the most fun. We played without any sidelines or boundaries, keeping the ball in the net of the crosse to avoid it being knocked out by an opponent! All this, of course, takes place at full speed. Often came calls of "Good!" or "Well done" or "Very nearly excellent", and even on one occasion "Very nearly international"! All those shouts came over the open pitch on the way to the goals, into which the players attempted to hurl the ball from out of the crosse. The goals are rather like smaller football goals.

Every day was not the same, and on one memorable day out I attended one of the many ceremonies to celebrate the rebuilding and reinstatement of Coventry Cathedral. Separate services were held – first of all for the men and women who designed and built the new centre of worship, then in turn for members of the armed forces, the clergy, and the students of the colleges. I was thrilled to be asked to be the representative for our student group!

Later I had the pleasure of taking my mother and her weekend guest to view the whole building and of course I still remember my mother's reaction to the huge tapestry designed, I believe, by Graham Sutherland, and the baptistery window designed by John Piper.

Later still, I took friends from Hungary to see the resurrected cathedral, parts of which brought tears to my eyes, and still do!

Modern educational dance (MED to us) was one of the reasons for my agreeing to take the year's course. When I originally qualified as a teacher, MED was a comparatively unknown item, and for me it was not the best dance form! However, it grew on me owing to the approach and methods of the tutor concerned. I remember the group being given tunics in four colours, representing water (blue), earth (green), fire (orange) and air (red), and we moved in four groups to create a free-flowing sequence to represent the four elements of life, intertwined and interdependent.

When this part of the course reached the point of examination we each had to produce a five-minute solo dance based on a choice of 'directions'. I clearly remember Marion Jones (a fellow teacher from Birmingham) choosing the theme music of the film *Exodus* for her solo as she chose a theme of 'vertical lines' around which to build her offering. I'm cross that at this moment I can't remember my own music, on which I based my theme of 'diagonals with pulses'. The music was from a recording I had made – believe this or not – in a Swiss hotel during a pre-dinner pause in the lounge bar. It haunted me for days. The band played it and played it at my request all the while I was mentally drafting out a sequence of movements. At last I seemed happy about this area of dance, which came in very useful during the inevitable teaching practice.

Another area which appealed to me was track and field, and for my assessment I had started writing a book on athletics and the teaching of athletics. We covered most events, then specialised in one of choice. Mrs Young, an anatomy and physiology specialist, found me a willing student – thanks to my mother (when I was little) and Mr Stamatakis at Loughborough I had a great interest in how we are put together. The book I put together became my constant point of reference later on. For the testing stage I chose hurdling as a specific item, and I not only analysed movements through having a fellow student hold different positions, but I had the book at the side of the track while coaching. All was OK – another string to my bow.

During the summer term we all had to face the acknowledgement of official bodies – i.e. regarding tennis (LTA) and athletics (AAA) tests, which we took at schools in Coventry, overseen (or examined) by officials of the two sporting bodies.

Every morning I set out at six thirty in my little Morris Minor 1000 to meet up in time for whatever the day held for us, and each evening I reached home at any time between nine and eleven thirty to catch up with my notes of the day's activities.

When teaching practice started, the school (Tudor Grange Girls' Grammar School, under the care and direction of Mrs Smith, the headmistress) was halfway to college on my route. Very lucky! I was there for two to three weeks, working with the head of department, Ms Avril Williams, who was the Welsh national javelin champion at that time.

The school and I were purposely matched up because by then I was happy to introduce the subject which had been the condition of my time at Canley – modern educational dance. Keen though

I was on the dances of Eastern Europe (particularly Hungary) and Israel, I introduced MED to girls who were hungry for what I could offer them. We even created a lunchtime club, which was well received by the school and my own lecturers. When she paid a visit to check on how things were getting on, Mrs Smith (the headmistress) was most supportive. She even came to the swimming baths with my classes, and ultimately offered me a post at Tudor Grange. However, I had given my word that I would return to Moseley! That didn't happen, though, as a new young teacher had been appointed during my absence! I would have been very happy to stay at Tudor Grange, but a promise is a promise – broken, but not by me!

Occasionally at weekends I took two of my student classmates home. We had a huge empty extra bedroom in the flat at King's Norton, and they found a visit a good way of achieving a bit of space away from the college.

Having achieved the object of my year at Canley, it was full steam ahead to the next stage, where I would be teaching for the next twenty-two years!

One part of the Canley year involved working with a noted mountain specialist for a week at Plas y Brenin – an activities centre in Snowdonia. There we hill-climbed, rock-climbed, canoed and generally exhausted ourselves learning the techniques of rock and water skills. It was a wonderful week, made even better for me by an agreement reached with Marion. She hated the rock section (we were tutored on some very severe climbs) and I was not so happy with swimming. As we both agreed that she would most likely teach youngsters water skills and I would teach youngsters rock-climbing skills, I ended up doing double rock work and she did double water skills. It worked out well as I had had a good grounding on Derbyshire gritstone climbs with Ken.

After all the time spent on the Canley course, I was set fair to achieve my dream, having fulfilled the objectives of our physical-education peers on the panel of Birmingham's education committee.

CHAPTER X

YARDLEY GRAMMAR SCHOOL

It was 1964.

I had to be formally interviewed, of course, at Yardley Grammar School, and, being forewarned that the headmaster, Mr W. A. Jenkins, was very much a classical scholar, I presented myself very formally attired. He even commented on my appearance and demeanour very politely and kindly!

All went well and I was appointed as teacher in charge of girls' physical education. I must admit that the position also gave me a slight financial lift. With my newly acquired qualifications in athletics and tennis, I had, it seemed, a wider range of skills than my predecessor, and by now I had a reasonable amount of experience in the subject of MED, so (apparently) desired by the authorities.

My arrival at Yardley Grammar School caused some comment – I had driven up in a two-seater Triumph Spitfire, which I could drive open-topped if the weather allowed.

Shown round the school, noting en route the facilities both for gymnastics and dance, and the hall with a first-floor balcony on either side, I was very impressed. I'd done the right thing. I had a very welcoming introduction to the school of my dreams.

At this point I was still somewhat apprehensive about the school, but each week I had teaching contact with every age group of girls, from eleven to eighteen years old, and settled in well.

I had a smallish room with a desk and chairs, also a shower and toilet. This was over the gym, up the stairs which led to the girls' changing room and showers. Later I even had a phone installed, which was shared with the PE master next door. It sat on a ledge in a hole in the wall, giving us both access and communication.

It had become a habit for those in the sixth form who had formed a guitar group to bring their instruments for storage in my cool washroom. Few of them had hard cases, and leaving them there helped to keep the instruments cool. At lunchtime, when the seniors met in their common room, they would come and collect their instruments.

On one memorable occasion Penny Hill came for hers, and before leaving my office she casually strummed a chord in passing.

"Stop. Please do that again!"

She looked a bit puzzled, but did so, and I asked her to show me how to make that rich, melodious chord. It happened to be A minor – a chord which not only struck me strongly, but was the reason for me to go and buy a guitar in town. It was a cheapish model, quite simple, but good enough for a beginner, and I promised myself I'd get a better one if I managed well enough with this one – made in Norway. I had some help from the group and made a soft case with a pocket for papers out of red deckchair canvas. I loved it, and in what little time I had at home I studied it with help and written notes from the girls, and a how-to book included when I bought the guitar.

Of course MED was added to the lessons I took, and if I remember rightly each class of girls had a gymnastics session, a hall (dance) session and a longer outdoor games and athletics session (depending on the season) each week.

Youth-hostelling was very popular with both girls and boys from, I think, the third form up to the sixth form. Our guitars usually went along with us, along with copious song sheets – not just for us, but also for the fellow hostellers we met and spent evenings with. Stan Butler, head of woodwork at Yardley Grammar School, was usually the organiser of these trips to, for example, the Peak District, where, as I understand it, there was usually a ceremonial burial of boys' caps – those boys who had by then officially left school and were looking forward to university life.

My most memorable YHA trips with them were both in Ireland. The first thing we did on landing from the ferry was to take all the boys – plus girls if they so wished – around the Guinness brewery. We hoped it would put them off, but I don't think it did. For myself, I just could not tolerate the half-inch foam at the top of the glass. Other memorable visits included the hostel at Agagavenna (I'm not sure of the spelling), where the warden was happy to reduce the chores we were normally expected to do. A horse ride up a steep mountain track was another experience for some, but most of the staff walked it! Coming down was quite exciting as the horses, sensing home, picked up speed to such a pitch that I could actually see a £1 note working its way out of the back jeans pocket of the boy riding in front of me. We all loved the open spaces, and I remember one evening, having done my stint of watch duty and being relieved by a colleague, I made my way to join the other staff at the village pub, from where the view of the sunset across the Atlantic turned all of us into poets.

After working very hard in all PE activities, summer came, and with it the annual sports day. Members of all the houses of the school (I'm afraid I forget their names) competed for individual awards and also for the overall championship trophy. This was a huge bronze copy of the world-famous *Discobolus*, mounted on a wooden base, and it was eagerly competed for.

It was always a very full programme, organised mainly by the boys' PE master, and it often brought some really spectacular results.

Teaching in the area of the high- and long-jump pits, where a few yards away a factory wall was the northern boundary of our 'stadium', I had developed a means of helping the girls in these events with almost life-sized pin figures in chalk on the wall. It certainly helped them to see what I was talking about!

One after-school event stands large in my memory. The PE

Mrs Eileen Carradine, 1974. Always available to help! My dear colleague and senior mistress at Yardley Grammar School.

Our Mrs Lancett, without whom we would have been lost, 1982.

Senior dance group, 1982. The Village He (the Old Man) Grew Up in.

Junior dance group, 1968. Shepherd boys ready for a stick dance.

The Wedding Party *in rehearsal.*

Visiting a day centre, Joy and group, Yardley Grammar School.

teacher from one of our district schools (we met at inter-school matches, and her husband was our head of metalwork) asked me, as they didn't have their own track, if she could bring a very promising girl for a session on ours. Immediately on meeting her, I felt there was tremendous potential in her. She and our team of sprinters would share training sessions.

My assistant at the time was (like me) from the north-east of England and had still a lovely (to me, anyway) Geordie accent. To this day, I can hear her, competing and well behind the others, calling out to me twenty yards away, "Sybil, did you see that? Did you ever see the like? Did you see it?"

The visiting girl's teacher made the necessary enquiries, and Sonia Lannaman was accepted into the Harriers. She regularly trained with the GB team, and in 1972 that supreme athlete was first included in our GB Olympic team. A plaque in the entrance hall of her school bears witness to her winning an Olympic gold or silver medal, I'm not sure. We were all thrilled for her – for her progress, and for her success!

CHAPTER XI

SCHOOL SKI TRIPS

As a keen skier, roundabout 1966 or 1968 I organised the first ski trip for boys and girls from the third form upwards.

As well as the normal arrangements with the rep of the travel company we used, which met our needs, I remember spending the summer holiday preparing booklets of information for each member of our group – and one for the headmaster for reference. Our deputy head, Mr Young, came as the required male adult, and his charming daughter, Mandy, was a good support. We travelled by bus all the way, the bus coming with us via the Channel crossing and on to our destination. The group studied their booklets, including the details of what to pack, and the questions which they would be given time for between afternoon ski school and the evening meal! It was, after all, a school trip! Information about where we were, what we saw en route and even the registration of Austrian cars was all to be filled in – all to remind them that we were in a foreign country which had its own traditions.

The first task was to get ourselves fitted with boots and skis at the local ski centre. A slight problem arose over the size of the boots Mr Young needed, but as a very tall (and dignified) adult he took it in good spirits.

We all appeared tidily for dinner that evening, and from where I sat I saw some puzzled expressions regarding the amount of cutlery in each place setting – not surprising really, for few of the boys and girls at their ages would have been used to table service and such.

However, I was amused to hear the head boy tell his table of youngsters (very quietly), "Just wait and see what Miss Chapman does."

That young man – John Prince – was still pleasingly in his senior position! He was invaluable also with regard to a student from Anstey College of Physical Education who had been allowed to join the party, hoping to study 'young people's approach to and enjoyment of a new sport'. This was part of her reason for joining us. When she became poorly, he took great care of her as she wasn't a good traveller.

The mornings were for ski school, and in the afternoons I took over to revise the morning's skills (mostly how to stop) and I would introduce the next day's work, which would be about changing direction.

There was a little shop in the village, and soon after our arrival a youngster came to tell me she'd forgotten her flannel. Off the two of us trooped – necessarily hand in hand – up the very icy slope to the shop. I think her name was Bernadette or some similar sweet Irish name. She was a pleasure to go shopping with. The kit list had included warm, serviceable boots, and her brothers, who had clubbed together so their little sister could come with the party, had apparently misunderstood and bought her a very nice pair of knee-high fashion boots. However, with a few almost slips we got there, and I taught her her first German words: "*Bitteschön, haben-sie eine Waschlappen?*" ("Please, have you a facecloth?") She was very pleased. Job done! Back she went to the grind of paperwork before dinner.

On an expedition to a major town for shopping she managed to buy a lovely very large shawl/scarf for either her mother or her grandmother. I'm sure the recipient loved it – a bit of Austria!

There were many ski excursions over the years that I was at Yardley: Italy, Austria, Bulgaria, etc., Bulgaria being one of the best trips. On one trip Bob Currier, the metalwork master, brought his two children and his wife (whom I knew well from inter-school matches). It was his wife who had brought Sonia Lannaman to our track.

Food was always plentiful and nourishing, so that was no worry, but on one occasion no fewer than four dishes of red-cabbage salad were parked on our table. "Well, we don't know it" or "Never had it at home" were a couple of comments, and someone replied, "Just look around and you'll see all the locals have survived very well!" End of problem!

Everyone had fun and enjoyed their ski lessons. Sometimes Bob and I left them in the capable hands of the instructors and went some distance away to just enjoy the skiing ourselves. Then came lunch, followed by our working with the group. Not many grumbles either, though some had a few aches to work off.

Occasionally a child might need a little mothering, and on one occasion I was helped by Mrs Lancett, mother of one of the girls in the school. I realised that one of the younger boys needed a lot of TLC in every way. He was gentle and quiet, but oh so worried all the time. Out on the slopes, I quite often escorted him to a rocky outcrop or hedge for toileting because I had been made aware by my very kind motherly colleague that there were sometimes accidents through nervousness. He was a very nice child and spent quite a time on occasions being looked after and put right by my caring colleague. In the end, I think he really enjoyed the break from home.

There were also some negatives as well as positives. On one occasion the necessary male member of staff was not aware of what was involved, and it wasn't made clear to him when he was included in the ski party. On the Channel crossing a few of the party spent time on deck and a few in the stuffy saloon playing cards. I thought the journey was going well, but when the message was passed for parties to be prepared to go below, where cars and coaches were parked, I had to look for my colleague. I found him stretched out on a divan in – yes – the ladies' lounge. I won't repeat our short conversation, but there was no doubt in my mind as to where he should have been! Worse was to come. Although I hesitate to deride a member of my own profession, it should be noted that on one occasion I had to ask the head boy and another boy to escort the said teacher (we were in a hotel at the time) to his room, loosen his clothes, and come back to the rest of us, whose enjoyment of the village band had been so rudely interrupted by the nearly legless drunken man who had a habit of wandering off!

That was the only real blot on the whole series of ski parties I organised. In hotels or inns where we stayed, sometimes there would be another school or university group, and one of the latter left free by their tutors caused quite a problem. I can honestly say that our behaviour never wavered from knowing the right thing to do, sometimes in the least-expected situations.

Bulgaria has developed tremendously in its development of excellent ski centres – we actually went twice with Bob and me as staff in charge. I had to warn all the boys and girls not to even think about pleasing any Bulgarian member of staff (waiters, etc.) by exchanging money and told them what the consequences would very likely be! The very first morning, after breakfast, one boy admitted quietly to me that, yes, the waiter had tried it on. He was a sensible lad, but all these years later I cannot bring his name to mind.

Bulgarians love children and the soft drinks on their dinner tables were very quickly replenished without even being paid for. We tried, but "No – the children are so happy" seemed to be the automatic response.

One morning one of our boys, for some unknown reason, refused point blank to get into the cabin of the ski lift when it arrived. Despite all of Bob's and my requests, and even pleas, he still refused as the lift queue grew longer and longer. He was a tall, well-built and powerful youth, but when Bob, so exasperated, faced him with "You daffodil!" he subsided into a nearby snowdrift and would not budge! Annoyed as we were, the Bulgarians in the queue thought it hilarious! I will say no more on the subject! I wonder if Bob remembers the occasion.

Although we had passes for the chairlifts at the top (beyond the cabin lift), many a time a boy or girl would be accompanied by a ski instructor – quite a thrill for them, but, as I have already said, the Bulgarians love children. Ours from Yardley seemed extra-special.

There were, of course, occasional mishaps, but none that could not be dealt with at the time.

These school ski trips were so exciting for the boys and girls we took. I hope they too remember them.

My own holiday skiing usually took place during the Easter holiday period, and usually I agreed that my friend with whom I had shared a flat came too. She was a great artist with a camera, and her photographs of tiny flowers growing and flowering within an icefall (frozen waterfall) were very expertly done.

In 1964, when I moved on to Yardley, tired of lining the pockets of a distant landlord, we had agreed to pay out on a mortgage for a house being built here in Worcestershire, where I still live, but Marie died a few years ago when living near Ross.

Referring back to skiing, I usually organised a pre-skiing-holiday meeting with the children's parents, and also a post-skiing meeting.

On one occasion after perhaps our very first trip, during the post-skiing meeting I asked the group what their greatest impression had been, and I think it was Louise who shot up her hand and exclaimed, "Oh, Miss, the peace!"

"Now that", I said to the parents, "was worth every penny."

However, a later pre-skiing meeting took a rather strange turn. Given a chance to ask me questions, one father requested very specific information: "Bulgaria, Miss Chapman? Bulgaria again? A country of Eastern Europe – a communist country – is there any particular reason?"

"Yes, there is, Mr ----- [long pause]. It is because your pound is virtually elastic at this time!"

He said nothing more, but I know his daughter felt rather embarrassed.

CHAPTER XII

THE WORLD OF WINES

Apart from winter holidays, I had for a long time had a deep interest in wines. For my twenty-first birthday I took my friend Delia and her sweet mother out for dinner to a hotel in Birmingham. Asked by the waiter to name our wine of choice, I was somewhat puzzled. He suggested a white from Germany for our fish course. OK! Later he removed the empty bottle and returned after a little while bearing the label and the collar from the bottle on a napkin as they dried and wished me a happy birthday. It was my first foray into the wine world. The collection of labels started that very evening and went on for many years.

Later both Marie and I, living in the flat and teaching in our respective schools, started to explore this unknown world of wines and made very judicious choices with the help of a German company through attending their advertised visits to hotels where 'tastings' were given in a most entertaining way. These occasions were also very informative. Occasionally a representative held a tasting in the house we had by now moved into. On these occasions we included neighbours and friends and had a very sociable party. Any wines ordered that evening were ultimately delivered to my garage (avoiding multiple delivery charges). From there they were collected, having all been prepaid.

My interest increased by leaps and bounds.

At one time, in Canada with my mother, I managed to find a bottle of her favourite dessert wine, and at this point, realising

I was truly interested in the subject, she told me, "You know, darling, your grandpa kept a very good cellar."

Having experienced the sometimes unhappy results of Dad's drinking, she had not told me about Grandpa until she was sure that I approached good wines with knowledge and control.

My interest in and knowledge of wines increased. I do enjoy talking to the reps of the wine company which, for me, is the very best there is. Whether in seriousness or encouragement, the cellar manager of the company usually adds 'MW' to my name on the box label every three months. We don't by any stretch exceed the government's recommended levels for drinking wine, and most often I drink the wine with dinner guests!

Finally, Marie and I went to Germany – this was in the days when you didn't have numbered seats on the plane, but instead passengers poured out of the gate to the plane with no thought of others. On this occasion, having my left arm in a sling still, from some rather worrying surgery, I managed to get to the front and secured two seats for us.

While in hospital, I always was aware that the surgeon when he did his ward round took more interest in the books on my bed than in his patient! If the books were to do with wine, they were gifts from my colleagues at school; but those on dance were ones I'd brought back from Russia, where we holidayed just before I went into hospital.

Another memorable occasion occurred when a group of pupils (third to sixth form) left a very entertaining picture in my mind. That evening, the boys and girls having retired for the night, I was in the bar when a group of three local musicians came in. One of them was 'wearing' a small dulcimer on a strap around his neck – it reminded me of the old days when cinema staff would enter the cinema during an interval with a large tray held by a strap around their necks, bearing ice creams to sell to the audience!

The musician with the dulcimer – quite a small one – played a tune or two then put the instrument down on a table. It was too good an opportunity for me to miss! Picking up the hammers I played a tune that will always remind me of my initiation into Hungarian dance – 'Pést Megyi Lássu és Friss Csardas' ('Slow and Quick

Csardas from County Pest'). It was the first Hungarian dance I learnt during Magda's first visit to our Society for International Folk Dancing (SIFD) summer school! As the musician came over to talk to me, the door of the bar opened and in the doorway stood Susan Mullis in pyjamas and dressing gown! She was a tall, slim teenager of our group, and she was a member of the school dance group!

I'll always remember her words: "Who's playing our music?"

Apparently her room was above the bar. She was a very sensitive girl, liked by all, and she just couldn't resist coming down to enquire. I was so pleased to explain the situation to those around me, and they smiled and applauded as Susan went back to her room.

A quick trip to France was interesting, but could not rival the tree-clad slopes rising from the river valleys in Germany or Plodiv, Bulgaria, in all their autumn glory.

Bulgaria was a total surprise – more surprising and more interesting from the point of view of both the people and the wines, and also their modern equipment for cold fermentation – viewed from the balconies.

I had already skied with, and sometimes without, school parties, and this trip outdid all others.

When Marie and I agreed to take the opportunity of being included in a dedicated wine visit to Bulgaria, one vintage time, it opened so many doors for me that I can now remember most of the details. It was *vintage* time as opposed to *tourist* time. What a difference! There were ten of us altogether. Marie's brother and his wife came, as did a sailor and his partner. He was on leave and apparently couldn't find any other trip available! With us in the minibus there was of course our driver, a newspaper correspondent and, I believe, a photographer. There was also our fantastic guide, Lilia. Personally, I had never met such an interesting and helpful tour leader. Because by then my interest in international traditions, folk music and dancing were literally part of the air I breathed, this sort of environment had a lot to offer me. Each day we set off on visits to vineyards and processing areas, and at the end of the day the wines on the dinner table were those in which I had shown the greatest interest. Irena went out of her way to find for me what I was looking for. I don't speak any Bulgarian – often German will do – but speaking with her was so easy because her English was excellent. She treated us as VIPs and understood my own personal fascination with traditional national cultures.

CHAPTER XIII

INTERNATIONAL FOLK DANCE

When we arrived in Plovdiv for a few days, I asked if it would be possible to attend, as a spectator, a workshop of the local folk-dance club. Alas, they had cancelled their regular evening because there was a match between Bulgaria and Switzerland (I believe) – a World Cup match which most of the dancers (the men and boys particularly) wanted to see on television. Quite understandable! However, a couple of hours later she came to tell me they had agreed to hold the normal dance workshop that evening.

When we arrived, we found two boys had carried a television set to their changing room, and during our time there every so often one of them went to have a quick peep at it. Then they would quickly tell the group how the match was going. I was overcome in every way. The workshop went very well indeed, and all the members were happy to do this for me! The only blot was the very rude exit by two holidaymakers from the scene. The dancers' teacher knew that it wasn't a *performance* I wanted to witness, but a real, serious workout. I'll never forget it, or how happy the dancers were to know that a dance teacher from abroad was so interested in their traditions.

The next morning, Marie needed to stay in her room. She wasn't very well, so I went with Lilia, who had asked the curator of the ethnological museum to open up the museum especially for me. It was a really lovely collection, depicting the lives of people living in that area – normally closed outside the tourist season. How lucky can you be?

Costume of the Gorali region, Southern Poland – acquired in Zakopane, c.1976.

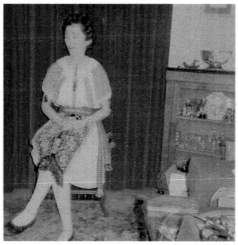

Back home from Romania.

The next morning, Marie felt well enough, and Lilia – bless her – got hold of the curator and the keys again so she also could enjoy their magnificent collection.

On the road a few days later, on our way to Sofia Airport, for our journey back to the UK, Lilia stopped the minibus at the steps of the Alexander Nevsky Cathedral without saying why we'd stopped! Out we got, and it's still so memorable an experience I can rarely talk about it without a tear or two. We walked up those wide steps and entered on the dot of eleven o'clock as the bells rang out and as the superb male-voice choir started singing the start of the service from above us, right round the domed ceiling-level balcony. It was a long time since I had heard anything so beautiful and so sincere! Yes, the tears flowed, and not just mine! What an experience with which to leave the country, but it wasn't to be the last time!

Farewells followed at the airport, and we took away wonderful memories to treasure.

Christmas arrived, and with it a large padded box from Bulgaria. Inside the box was a lovely letter from Lilia saying how much she had enjoyed meeting us and enclosing two LPs of 'Orthodox Bulgarian Music'. When I wrote to her to express thanks for her help, interest and hard work, I also said I would be skiing in Borovetz at Easter.

On the Saturday of our arrival, walking across to the ski lift, I saw two people coming my way and waving to me. Yes, it was Lilia and her sister (also a tour leader), who had taken two days from work and booked a simple cottage accommodation in order to spend some time with us! Her gifts – the copper tray (for glasses) and the lidded copper dish (for nibbles) – are now and always have been since I received them, the centrepiece on my dining table, and a 'forever memory' of a very lovely person.

A few years later we were in Bulgaria skiing again. Marie and I usually had a coffee at 11 a.m. on the veranda of a hotel near the ski lift. It has often happened that people we met have asked us if they may share our table (something the average English tourist neglects to do – I often notice they simply sit down if a chair is free, unlike tourists from other parts of Europe!).

So we met Rajka (j sounds as y) and her granddaughter, both of whom asked politely in German if they could join us. I shall refer to the youngster as Eevie. Eevie's grandfather was shopping and they had heard us speaking, and although they didn't speak English they explained that because of their history they were shy of sharing a table with German visitors. The first thing I did when I got back to school was to arrange a penfriend for Eevie – a girl of similar age in a class I was taking! Marie had learnt German at A-level, and I was just starting out with the language, for which I had a tutor at home. We had made yet another connection. Our coffee meetings with Rajka and Eevie became a habit over the ten days we were there.

The skiing was good, and the opportunities for photography were good. Just before we left we met Eevie's grandfather, Bogdan, who had brought drinks for us for the journey! From then on we kept in regular contact. I was so sad when a card came telling me of the death of Eevie's mother from a brain tumour. At that time I had just lost my sister Helen with a similar illness. It left Bogdan and Rajka completely without family or any support. Their granddaughter grew up to be a specialist in many languages and studied at college in Worms, Germany. There she lived and married and had a sweet child – a boy – the absolute apple of Bogdan's eye. Conditions worsened for Rajka and Bogdan, but he did manage some short periods with the boy. We kept in contact, but one Easter we didn't receive the usual Easter greeting, so I wrote to them both and learnt that the political situation had changed considerably! Democracy had reared its head! The first letter I received told me all I needed to know: his pension had been reduced to about fifty euros and hers to forty euros monthly. That was in *euros*, to pay for rent, water, gas, electricity and food. I still have all their letters, and rereading them hurts me so much. What could I do? He had been a highly thought-of engineer; she had been the répétiteur of the national dance company (full-time musician/pianist). What could I do? "Nothing" came the reply. Anything posted would be 'lost' en route.

After a few weeks, during which I thought and thought and

thought the situation through, finally I felt compelled to go and see the situation myself! I'd read so many times their written invitations, including 'There is always room here for you.' So I went, although I of necessity came through customs in a wheelchair, and I soon spotted them holding up a huge placard: 'Sybil'. I recognised him by his corduroy worker's cap, and she too looked so very different from the days when we met for coffee at the ski resort.

They took me by taxi to the simple hotel I had booked, where Bogdan insisted on checking it over to make sure it was OK. On the way out he asked the receptionist to get me a taxi later, to spend the evening with them. Then we went to their apartment. I have travelled widely in Eastern Europe, but I was totally dismayed when we reached their home. The outside of the block of flats was totally uncared for. There was a rusty main door, and a doubtful lift took us to the floor below theirs, where we first visited a neighbour. Her apartment was pristine and lovely, with very well-cared-for period furniture. I think they really wanted their guest to meet this lady, who had been, and still was, a great support for them. Then we continued up to the next floor. Their poverty was visible from the start. The neighbour had made a dish for them which merely needed Bogdan to heat it up. I'm not really an eater of lasagne, but the neighbour joined us at dinner time and I was so relieved to see they had some support. Another friend joined us who had a tiny bit of English; otherwise all chatter was in German.

When it was time for me to go back to the hotel, the taxi was ordered and paid for in advance despite my protestations when I was being so lovingly escorted.

The next day they both came to collect me for a walkabout in the city, Sofia. The market was excellent – though we all hurried past a tempting butcher's stall! I bought a good pair of gloves as I'd left mine in the car at Gatwick Airport. All our conversation was now in German, translated for Rajka by Bogdan. There was a superb and spotless workers' canteen below ground, and it was very welcome! I insisted it was my treat, and we all had a spectacular lunch of chicken casserole. Not until Bogdan had given Rajka the utensils she needed to use, and I saw the care he took in helping her to remove and later put back on her coat and hat, did I realise she wasn't very well. Sadly, it seemed to me that there might be the start of Alzheimer's disease.

The next thing we did – and it's quite normal in that country – was to sit in on not one but two wedding ceremonies. They were lovely, and the music was very soothing to all three of us.

I had taken for them, as gifts, some of my own weaving – a couple of lambswool scarfs, which they loved.

That night I dined on warmed-up lasagne – they on bread and cheese! I had managed to escape for a few minutes to get some cash, which, when it came to farewell hugs, I managed to deposit in Bogdan's jacket pocket. The next day, regretfully, I was to return home. They took me to the airport and we shared a tearful farewell. They had, though, given me the phone number of Eevie at university in Germany.

Sometime later she very generously and kindly gave me her bank reference numbers, so once I was at home I could take some action even though it couldn't be much. It made it easier to have this form of contact as, however little I'd sent, Eevie's boyfriend (but never she) could take it to her grandparents very shortly afterwards. She hated what the country had become.

Sometime later in one of his so affectionate letters Bogdan told me that they had both managed to get new coats and shoes for the winter – their first new things in twenty-five years! As ever, his letter ended, "*mit eine tausend Küssen*", which I'm sure the reader will understand.

A few months later, Rajka was in a nursing home, and Bogdan, so kind and generous a man, was hoping I could visit again, but by then I was back in hospital for a hip replacement. When Rajka died he wrote to tell me that he was moving to Switzerland (I think it was) as by then his lovely granddaughter, her husband and Bogdan's beloved great-grandson had space there to care for and look after him.

About three years later, when Bogdan and I had sent many, many letters to each other (always with a thousand kisses), Eevie phoned to tell me that he had died and to thank me for the love and care I showed her family.

Originally, I had learnt German because of ski parties and my own holidays in Austria, etc. My tutor, Frau Rubenstein (originally from Vienna) had been taking an evening class which I had joined, then later she offered me one-to-one sessions at her home. I had found with the school groups that at least one of the party should be able to ask for bread and cheese or something at 9 p.m. for the hungry teenagers I was supporting.

In Poland we met Maria – such a sweet but overworked rep and guide. Marie and I flew out to Warsaw then on to the small town of Zakopane in the hills. It is situated in a beautiful basin, out of which run valleys reaching up Kasprowy Mountain. One of these valleys is quite rightly called Crocus Valley (in English). Our aim was, as ever in beautiful surroundings like these, to ski. However, the snow did not fall heavily enough, so we spent a lot of time exploring this lovely area. Our guest house was delightful – the outer walls of massive pine trunks were sealed with yards and yards of tarred rope. Very, very traditional and so beautiful! Our room was a huge attic and my skis stood in a corner, never used, as it happened, but there was so much to enjoy that it didn't bother us. The market was a regular joy.

Our hotel didn't have a bar, but there was a sort of robbers' hideaway up in the forest, where, being seen approaching and knocking on the great door, we were met by a 'brigand' (dressed accordingly) holding aloft a huge axe-like weapon. He welcomed us in, and there, in the centre of the hideaway, a ten-foot-diameter low wall surrounded a fire pit. Over the fire, from a tripod, hung a large kettle. On a table nearby were large glasses, seemingly half filled with water. We were offered tea and chunks of bread and cheese, then the glasses were filled from the kettle in which the tea had been boiled. We didn't at first realise that the water in the glasses was in fact vodka. Very, very welcome after the climb through the trees! Also quite habit-forming!

In the market we could buy some lovely things, but most often we bought, very cheaply, what looked at first like shelled hard-boiled eggs. These turned out to be cheeses! With them and for fifty pence a half-litre were bottles of vodka, plus equally cheap but good-to-drink bottles of apple juice. These we would take back to our temporary home, where on the landing outside our room there was a sort of small lounge. There we would meet and share our aperitif offerings with a young couple with whom we shared a dining table; sometimes we managed to persuade Maria to join us.

We met her sometimes outside and went together to a little coffee house. On one occasion we met and she looked so very tired and worried. Apparently she'd had a call from an English visitor to go to the Kasprowy Hotel – what for, she didn't know, but she was very grateful for our suggestion to accompany her over the very steep meadow to see what this person was yet again complaining about. We waited in the hotel lounge for Maria's return. She was very depressed – amongst other complaints was the lack of snow! Stupid, thoughtless, but nevertheless worrying for our Maria!

Some English tourists, I've often noticed, will complain about everything – just because it's different.

We took a trip to a big farmers' market where they bought and sold livestock, and our coachman, in full peasant costume, took pleasure in introducing his new English friends to his colleagues. He was the one who once or twice drove us up Crocus Valley.

One day, after reading a poster nailed to a tree, I asked Maria if she could get us tickets for a folk-dance performance in the village hall a couple of days ahead. She knew my interests and my work very well, but was surprised that we knew about the folk evening. Time, date and place was all we needed, I explained: because of the picture on the poster!

The next evening found in the front row of the hall. Our two friends were just behind us and all the rest were at the back of the auditorium. Halfway through, in the interval, Maria appeared in the aisle gesturing to me, so I got up to see what she wanted. Would we like her to make an appointment to meet the director/ teacher of the folk group? Would we!

The next afternoon we were escorted (just the two of us) to the small bus station, where in his office, as manager of the local transport system, we met the dance leader. A little card I had with me with our West Midlands branch of the Society for International Folk Dancing logo on it was of immediate interest to this very friendly gentleman. I told him, with Maria as translator, what my work entailed, and when he mentioned costume I told him I had already a traditional blouse and petticoat. He left us for a few minutes, then returned with a beautiful skirt and bodice/waistcoat to complete the outfit, but he would not allow me to pay anything. Then he asked about the traditional shoes – no, I didn't have them. He left again and returned with a pair of their lovely locally made shoes in a very solid leather with straps which criss-crossed the lower legs. What a wonderful gesture! Later he would go to return the typewriter he'd brought in from the next office, on which he had typed out permission for these items to be taken abroad. He'd already refused any payment, but I thought that when he took the machine back, after our departure, he would find what I thought to be about the correct amount of zlotys, which I'd slipped under it when his attention was distracted by Maria (she knew what I was about to do).

Then came our departure, and in farewell Maria gave Marie and me each a notepad about five inches by three fixed within a beautiful hammered-pewter cover depicting the tower of Krakow. I know from a letter she sent that she was actually writing to us to thank us for our kindness and concern while she awaited the arrival of her next group of tourists.

Some days later I received a letter from the dance leader himself, in which he told me that if I didn't have a coral necklace, which should be worn with their regional costume, I should let him know so that he could send me one. The letter was translated for me by a university colleague of a member of our dance group, and a reply for me to send was likewise translated into Polish. He was such a true gentleman, and the whole holiday still lives with me – and on my kitchen wall!

CHAPTER XIV

HUNGARIAN DANCE

A two-centre visit to Romania – seaside and mountains – happened one summer with a friend, Anthea, whom I'd got to know well when she joined the West Midlands group. As a teacher, musician and classical singer, she soon found herself in the demonstration group.

Our first stop was at a coastal resort, where we came almost face-to-face with the tragedies created by changes in national borders, which happened, I believe, after the Second World War when something like a third of Hungary was lost to Romania. Put simply, thousands of Hungarians were forced to consider themselves Romanians, lost their houses, their land, their work and were forced into high-rise flats with dreadful facilities and industrial work. Damn Ceauşescu!

At the seaside where we went every morning there was an elderly couple with a stall selling handwork to visitors. I bought a lovely handmade straw hat and a lovely piece of decorated (all-white) linen, which lives now in my dining room. When I heard them talking to each other, I realised they were really Hungarian, and the next day on our arrival at the beach I greeted them politely and happily in Hungarian! I think at that moment the sun beamed even more brightly for both of them. They wanted me to buy a blouse I'd been examining, but I knew it was too small. I tried to explain that, lovely though it was, they must sell it to someone else. The man did realise I was right, and it would have been silly for me to buy it. I told him, helped by signs and actions, that someone else would be sure to want to buy it, and he understood that I was aware of his situation and at the same time in great sympathy with their position. We smiled and communicated from then on each day.

Anthea and I then went on in a few days to Braşov – a lovely old town where history revealed itself. We spent the next week in Poiana Braşov – in the mountains, where one memorable evening we went out in a group to look for brown bears. The forest was up a steep hill opposite our hotel, and while waiting quietly we were rewarded by the sight of a mother bear leading two cubs and sniffing around for anything edible! Of course, inevitably, one member of the group was unwise enough to use a flash camera and they all ran away – but it could easily have become a bad situation. Some British tourists just don't think!

Looking towards the hotel, below and opposite where we were, in bright moonlight we saw a huge bear approach the kitchen rubbish skip, after opening the gate to it! We saw him climb up quite clearly, and heard him rummaging around amongst bottles, cans and other rubbish. Then we saw him leave the skip and amble off back up the hill through the still-open gate.

A father and young son had decided to go back to the hotel before the rest of us. When we met up with them they were both shaking. Walking down the road to the hotel, the father and son had been pushed aside by a huge bear also making for the hotel. After passing between them, it had simply gone on its way, leaving them to follow on! What a memory for one small boy!

One evening we all went down to Braşov itself to the theatre, where there was to be a folk-dance and music performance. Knowing I was on the lookout for a girl's costume, our guide went backstage and arranged with one dancer, who was also a singer, that our guide would make an arranged gesture during her part in the performance if her costume was what I was looking for (because each region has its own costume and details). Our guide would then take me to her after the performance. The costume was just what I wanted, but I hadn't brought cash to the theatre, so it was arranged that our guide would bring me to the theatre the next day. At the appointed time there she was, with the whole costume prepared, so the deal was done and it was ready for me to bring home, but I did have to go shopping for the headdress – rather like a shawl/veil. We managed to find one in a ladies' shop selling such things, and so the costume was now complete – and it has been used in demonstrations.

In 1967 in Yardley, in the staffroom, I happened to pick up a copy of our bulletin – a small résumé of what was going on in Birmingham schools: vacancies, exhibitions, courses, etc. There in front of me was an opportunity too good to miss. The summer school of the SIFD was to be held that year at Swansea University, and it would include Hungarian dancing in particular and possibly other dance forms from Poland and Israel, etc. I had to go to Swansea!

Magda Osskó (in formal terms I think her name is Osskó Endréné) was basically the second-in-command of the Institute of Culture in Budapest, and she would be teaching the Hungarian sessions. Without dwelling on 'college living', suffice it to say the student accommodation was excellent and the offerings in the dining hall were beyond reproach. The man in charge was Professor Jack Richardson, one of the founder members of our society and a professor of chemical engineering. It was he who sorted out visiting teachers' visas, etc.

I set out – by now with an open-top MG sports car in light blue – and made my way on a route known as the Heads of the Valleys Road. This was before most motorways had been built. It was a lovely day and that journey was to be repeated many times.

There were already quite a few people there when I arrived and checked in – some of them I was to keep as good friends for many years. That first morning of introduction to the traditional folk dances of Hungary was, for me, the opening of a door on to a new and wonderful world.

Magda, with a personal history of war and invasion after invasion, had had many occasions in her life which she could well have done without, but she had risen above all of it. Her indomitable spirit and her beliefs had carried her and her family through the worst that that period (the First World War onwards) could assail her with. Her family background was a noble one, as was her husband's. Her father, as aide-de-camp of the Emperor of the Austro-Hungarian Empire, was there at Sarajevo when the First World War started. Through thick and thin, and despite the problems of the time, she had managed not only to look after her family but to train, then work for them all. Despite all that lay behind in her history, her ability to help and encourage people never ceased.

On the second day of teaching she beckoned me to one side, where she explained that the following year she would be conducting workshops in Vác (a lovely little town further up the Danube from Budapest). It was open to all, whatever their background or circumstances, and she asked me if I would like to be included in the workshops.

At first I could not believe what she was saying, but it took little time for me to give her my answer. From that day until her death she was my most valued teacher and friend. I am in regular contact with her family – in particular her eldest daughter, who keeps me up to date between my now infrequent visits.

Magda met me, that first visit in 1968, at the airport and took me home, where we would spend a few days before the journey to Vác. Her husband, Endré, who was with the national bank, her two sons and her daughter were a delight to meet. At that time I spoke almost no Hungarian at all, but we got along just fine with English and a little German. The family apartment was quite spacious. Later on I also met her father – by now very aged, but, like all the men I have met there, very, very courteous and caring.

She had arranged that I would have a room in Vác with a colleague as she had to have a place where the girls and boys would be accommodated. We all lunched together in the gym where we 'worked'. Lunch was usually of fresh fruit bought from a nearby market. We had Zoli Bácsi (Uncle Zoli) as our *zenész* (musician). It is the custom to call a male teacher 'Uncle' and a woman teacher 'Aunt' (*Néni*) – in this case Magda Néni. The class was very mixed, and the people were so interesting to mingle amongst. One very tall man was a professor – I think, of maths. Some chaps were market porters. One young woman – Judit (pronounced Yudit) – was a primary-school teacher. Others worked in shops or offices. There would usually be about twelve to sixteen of us, if I remember correctly. Those days were miraculous to me – everyone was glad for me to be there and very kind to me, and non-critical regarding my lack of knowledge – up to now – of their traditional dance forms.

The memories come rushing by me as I write!

We covered children's dances, girls' dances, boys' dances and men's and couples' dances – and we never seemed to stop! Sometimes we'd have a male teacher – usually one of very high reputation, like the army instructor. There wasn't a dull moment or any lagging behind!

Once, when Magda had to take a quick trip home, I spent the evening in a local café bar, which gave me a chance to write home to my mother. I was using blue airmail stationery and seemed to keep attracting the locals' attention. In answer to their smiles I just smiled and nodded, not realising that the local evening paper had a whole paragraph about an English teacher being in Vác for the summer dance course!

Not surprisingly, Magda had taken me to the city before departing for Vác, and there I bought my first of many dance boots. After a hectic day of working in them, I sometimes had a problem in the night with cramp in my calves. I soon got used to it though, and they felt absolutely right on my feet. I still have that first pair!

One Sunday I was taken to the northern hills to visit a schoolmaster. On the way, winding above the very narrow road, we passed some children, each carrying a bag with clothes showing over the top. I arrived at the teacher's home to find that word had gone round that a local folk costume was being sought out by a visiting teacher!

I was given such a range from which to choose that I needed the teacher's help. I already had the boots, and now I acquired the complete costume, including a beautiful shawl and cap. Word had got round!

During the second week I had a lovely surprise. Unrealised by me, Magda had registered me with the police – as one did then. She appeared in the gym that day laden with a huge armful of gladioli, and she told me that lunch that day would be in the *Csárda* (bar)

Dancing for a church meeting – Douglas and me and a young dance group.

A performance in Budapest of one of Magda's groups, with which I spent some time.

Magda and Endré's fortieth wedding anniversary with Endré's school friend the cardinal of Hungary.

In the garden of the synagogue in Budapest – the weeping willow of remembrance.

opposite. Then she presented me with two genuine locally made coffee mugs! Everyone gathered round to wish me happy birthday – hugs and kisses from nearly everyone. I was ecstatic.

"How did you know?"

"When I took your passport, I saw the date! It's nice having a birthday, but not quite as good when you're not at home!" was her reply.

I was almost weeping, and the day is forever etched on my memory. Magda's kindness was without bounds, always, and those two mugs were the first items to be hung on my kitchen wall, top – centre.

Back I went to Budapest for a week or so, and I was very, very surprised when Endré took me on a city tour in an open-topped bus. So that he could describe what I was seeing without intruding on others, we sat right at the back of the bus. One exceptional picture stays in my mind of Russian soldiers in marching order, crossing the square in front of the city hall. Then marched diagonally across our intended path, as one, and all the heads in front of us were sharply turned to the side, away from the soldiers. I realised they were making a strong political gesture of dislike! It was, I'll admit, somewhat intimidating and it was a gesture I was to observe quite a few times when Russian soldiers were seen, in pairs, at places like railway stations. Endré also escorted me into the fantastic national bank – an architectural treasure!

The drive round the city was a splendid experience – so many historic events and styles were reflected in the buildings. One could say there was a similarity to other European capital cities – Prague, Vienna, Paris, etc.

The river – a busy throughfare for waterborne traffic – is very beautiful, and from the centre of Budapest one can see at least three majestic bridges spanning the water.

On Margit-sziget (Margaret Island), which is reached by a road which slopes down from the bridge, there is a lovely open-air theatre, and I was lucky enough to be taken to performances there by both the Polish and Hungarian state dance companies in turn. With lovely trees and bushes for a backdrop, and the moon and stars lighting the sky, both experiences were truly wonderful.

I was also taken to a rehearsal of the Hungarian state group and introduced to Rabái, the then teacher and director/producer of their fantastic dance theatre. Unforgettable!

I was gradually finding my way around, often on my own and sometimes with Magda or her husband. Buda, to the west of the river, stands high and strongly with the spire of the Mathias Church rising steeply in silhouette near the royal palace. The crest of the hill is surrounded by a strong wall – built centuries ago by the Fisherman's Guild as a protection against invasion. The ancient cobbled streets and the huge Trinity statue just beyond the welcoming arched doorway into the church add to the magic of this place, as did the spring blossom.

A MAGYARAZAT
(To Hungary)

I have loved Budapest, dearly and deeply,
Since that first morning – gold, white and pure;
The tall spire of Mathias I saw, rising steeply –
Over the Bastion that keeps her secure.

I had no thoughts, then, of music or moonlight,
I was a traveller – the guest of a week.
Yet, when they pointed – "The Danube at twilight",
Startled, I found there were tears on my cheek.

I have loved Buda, and now in deep friendship,
Here is my refuge, my solace, release.
Now – and in future – I think of her standing –
A history behind her; a prospect of peace.

Sitting so often in the kitchen while Magda cooked, I learnt to prepare quite a range of Hungarian dishes, which I still make here at home. The cafés and restaurants in Budapest are excellent – many dating back centuries, and some with descendants of the original owners still running them. I well remember the music shop where I bought my first paper copy of 'Himnusz' – the national song of the people, which is sung (I found) at the end of the 11-a.m. service in the churches.

Friends from England that I have shown around Hungary have experienced the wonderful atmosphere as – as one – the congregation stands to sing the words, with an organ playing the very wonderful music. The song is played and sung with such emotion and such a community spirit.

By the time Mrs Thatcher had the visa requirement removed, I already had nearly forty, in passport after passport, but up till then it had been reasonably straightforward to acquire one.

The workshops I attended (sometimes as many as three in a year) were held in some most interesting places – not only Vác, but Sopron, Debrecen, Szátmar and so on – all very memorable towns. Then on my return it was a case of a day's rest then a car ride to Swansea, Nottingham or Edinburgh, etc., etc., where there were branches of the SIFD waiting to dance Hungarian!

One year, in a chaotically rushed start to the journey to reach Hungary for yet another workshop, I had to rush to London, to the Hungarian visa office, and there I met a huge crowd of Americans seeking visas to continue their European tour. My heart sank – each one was being told, "Come back in twenty-four hours." I'd already managed to book a flight for the next day!

My name was called, and a very cooperative lady asked me the purpose of my visit. When I told her about the dance course, she smiled and said she too had learnt traditional Hungarian dances when she was younger. It just so happened that I had the business card in my pocket (from my previous visit) of Vásarhdy Lázslo, the chief of the Institute of Culture at that time and also one of my many teachers. The girl clapped her hands and told me he had been one of her teachers. Then she added some rubber stamps to my passport and visa and wished me a happy time! As I left, there was almost a chorus of "What's she got that we ain't got?" in strong American accents! I was nearly on my way – a quick flit home and the next morning I was off to the airport.

The workshops were so very rewarding – particularly getting to know about the teachers, their backgrounds, etc., etc. There was never a dull moment, though sometimes the heat got a bit too much. I remember dancing with a Norwegian and seeing, on the lovely wooden floor, a circle of dampness – the perspiration was dripping from our elbows it was so hot. When there was a pause, I dared not sit down because when I stood up again my soaked garments would be very obvious. However, there would be slightly sweetened lemon tea given out as a reviver. We usually worked in glass-sided gyms.

The Institute of Culture in Hungary is staffed, I believe, by teachers of the highest standard. Every workshop I was privileged to attend was tutored by specialists who each had a particular area of dance to pass on so happily to those attending. One was a specialist in the dance traditions of girls, women and children. Another was a specialist teaching the army group. So many European countries, including Russia, Hungary and, I think, Poland – have developed a choir and/or a team of dancers who travel and perform.

To know that you are working with a tutor who is among the top teachers in his or her area gives one the urge to work harder than hard. They were all time specialists, and the knowledge I acquired was very soon spread around our groups here in the UK, as well as in our school, where we gained quite a reputation for our performances. Dancing in day centres for elderly local people was always very rewarding – particularly when we sometimes found a spectator originally from one of the countries whose traditional dances we were performing.

I was very fortunate that I was allowed to attend these workshops at the Institute of Culture. Sometimes they took place during our school term time, not just in the school holidays.

Invariably I was the only foreigner. Those attending were from every walk of life, including students, shopworkers, (very importantly) teachers, and even young men who were market porters in the city. I made many friends there. One man was a professor of mathematics and a brilliant dancer.

I also attended teaching sessions and demonstrations in a particular junior school whose teacher, on my invitation, came to stay a while with me to see how teaching (in many subjects) was approached here. We're still in contact.

I visited many groups who had weekly sessions, and even

attended international competitions, thereby picking up lots of useful ideas on presentation.

Everyone – particularly the children – was thrilled to have a foreign teacher visiting them, and I was highly delighted to be joined here, in our West Midlands branch (Selpar), by two Chinese students who were studying at Birmingham University. When they had asked our international centre in London for help in finding a dance group, they were advised to find me, and joined us for the rest of their final term at university.

Now, following a visit their parents made to collect their two university sons to take home for the holiday – and a delightful reunion we had – at Christmas I found myself opening an *enormous* parcel they sent me as a Christmas gift.

Dance is a universal joy, and my years spent in studying this particular branch of the arts is in my mind at all times. It may interest the reader to know that the Hungarian dance csardas (pronounced chardash) originated in bars and wine houses, called a *csárda*. And the Hungarian equivalent of a disco, such as many of our youth visit, is a *tánc ház*. There dances of great energy are enjoyed with their own folk music and songs in a modern style.

Each time I returned from Hungary, I had copious notes to rewrite, tapes to listen to and usually a lovely piece of folk craft. After all the workshops I had taken, the SIFD helped me to open our own West Midlands branch. The authorities were contacted and provision was made at Selly Park School for our evening classes to start.

A few weeks and lots of enjoyment later, it happened that the Hungarian state dance group was to visit the Alexandra Theatre in Birmingham. Of course, yes was the answer when I suggested we all went to see the group in action. I knew what it was all about basically. The group was now calling itself Selpar, and it was an enormous enjoyment. The following Tuesday, one man in the group – Alf Garton, who had a job to do with printing – appeared with 100 sheets of headed A4 writing paper. The following week a lady of the class whose husband had something to do with metalwork appeared with some cards with small brooches attached, and the third week Rod appeared with a huge pile of T-shirts printed with our name and the logo of the state dance theatre. This I was a little dubious about, but when later I met Rabái and told him about this new group he agreed heartily to our sharing the logo, which had appeared on every single page of the programmes we had all purchased at the theatre that memorable Saturday night.

In 1973, shortly after the start of the West Midlands group, we organised an 'open event', and a coachload of friends and colleagues came from London to cheer us on and enjoy the opening. The officers of the society were very complimentary and encouraging, and from then on we frequently had visiting guests and got to know members of other groups by attending weekends away in many different towns and country places.

Ken Ward – the acknowledged specialist at that time of Balkan traditional dance – was invited to lead a workshop at the Billesley Hotel in King's Heath, on the south side of Birmingham.

And so we kept very busy – often at weekends.

At a workshop with Magda (centre) and
'pianist for the day' (far right), Rotherham, 1974.

CHAPTER XV

SCHOOL PERFORMANCES

After my first visit to Hungary, where I was made very much one of the family, I had come home with the determination to create a complete evening performance at school by our, by now, really good dance club.

Initially it was girls only, so we had to do a bit of pretending. Later came the boys to join them. For this first staging, the theme was to be a Hungarian–Polish wedding occasion.

Lower-school boys and girls sat on the steps leading up to the stage, from where they were to sing folk songs, leaving a space for the wedding guests, who danced through the aisles between sections of the seated audience. Sixth-formers worked the lights. My mother had sketched a village scene for the art department to transfer to the curved backing of the stage. The woodwork department had built an enormous picture frame near a table on which there were a few household items on a special folk-craft cover where I could write the order of events for the wedding party to follow. The lights dimmed, and one figure – actually the head girl – dressed as an old lady in one of my peasant costumes, picked out by a single light, proceeded to dust and tidy the tabletop. She picked up a small frame, dusted it, then looked longingly at it. A full beam searched out the enormous frame to reveal the wedding couple, brilliantly portrayed as they stepped forward – a Polish groom and a Hungarian bride, each holding an end of a large curved flower arch. The old lady left the stage and the guests danced into the hall, through the audience, and through the flower arch up on to the stage. What a party! They were all singing and handling (empty) wine bottles. José and Doreen as the bride and groom were spectacular, particularly as we hadn't had much rehearsal time.

Then the moment arrived when the bride came down to the floor of the hall, where the audience sat. José performed her solo – a dance of her own making – to a gypsy-band accompaniment. I thought it was absolutely superb. I had been asked by José (before the start and with a quick peep through the curtains) where my mother was sitting, and as she danced a lovely arrangement – all her own – she literally danced it to (and, I think, for) my mother. It was a gesture I have never forgotten.

After that, the party went on. Dances from Hungary and Poland were performed, and the show was completed with a very strong sequence of traditional recruiting dances, with singing in Hungarian by the team.

After the performance, quite a few parents made very appreciative comments about the wonderful efforts of everyone.

I was approached by the mother of one of the girls, and she asked me if there was any chance she could work with me. Later she, as pianist, visited various schools to accompany song or dance lessons and stated that this was what she had really longed to do. I discovered she was a really brilliant musician, and she ultimately helped me greatly with music theory for my guitar. She held highly esteemed qualifications from Glasgow's academy of music and was more than willing to spend time with us after school each Friday. We fell into a pattern. Her health wasn't too good, so I would drive her home after a dance workout with the group, and after a small meal she would play some of the music I asked for. Sometimes I would sing, or a colleague from another school would play a few recorder pieces with Mrs Lancett on the piano and me with a pair of drumsticks used both on the side of the television set and on a pile of newspapers. In this way we achieved some very interesting tapes for the other school, where Scottish dancing was popular. My colleague could also pass on some of the simpler pieces she worked on with me. It was she who taught me so much about harmony, etc. One summer I persuaded Mrs Lancett to enter a music competition, and she said she would if I would! So while I chortled away with my guitar, singing 'Scarborough Fair' to win that particular section of the competition, she won high praise with Bartok's Romanian Dances, from memory. Her music had been left with the judges!

From then on, many times, I helped her before leaving her house after our Friday-night 'lesson'. There was time to give her hands a therapeutic wax bath – I honestly don't know how she kept on playing with such pain. It's quite a well-known treatment, but difficult to attend to if one is on one's own!

Mrs Lancett often managed to come in for rehearsals during the dinner break as well.

Occasionally she came as my musician when I was asked to take Hungarian workshops for our branches elsewhere, and her playing was very much appreciated.

Quite frequently, the team and I were invited to a day centre where elderly or infirm adults would spend their time in company. This always required the headmaster's permission, of course. I drove most of the group in the school minibus, with the rest in a large car driven by Mrs Oxenbury, the mother of one of the dancers, who so very willingly offered to help in this way. Those afternoons served a multitude of purposes. It was certainly therapeutic for the elderly men and women, who so enjoyed these visits, and it was very good to see, in the interval, the communication of young and old together. On one occasion, one lady gave me a record she had; another donated a pair of Balkan costume socks for our wardrobe. The youngsters wore a selection of costumes I had imported and also some home-made pieces. I did seem to do a lot of sewing in those days!

The most memorable afternoon we spent – invited by a letter to our headmaster, which was passed on to me – was to the synagogue. We had already experienced their hospitality, but this was to be the last such occasion before I retired. Mrs Jaffa, the secretary, had asked for the first time for me to send her a copy of the programme in advance. The first part of the programme – of very, very energetic dances from Poland, Hungary and other countries of Central and Eastern Europe – was wonderfully received, and in the interval, as had become our custom, the dancers mingled with the audience. Many of the elderly gentlemen loved the petticoats, and the ladies loved the starched blouses and embroidered bodices. I might add that the programme I chose was geared to all (or almost all) the countries which members of our audience had left, or escaped from.

The second part of our programme started, and as the music came on there was literally a deathly hush. I had arranged a calmer choreography of my own which involved a 3/4 rhythm (waltz) with many different circles forming and re-forming, finishing in a simple waltz around the hall.

As the first bars of the music started, everyone, except for two people in wheelchairs, stood up and started to sing. This waltz tune brought back so many memories (good and bad) for all these lovely appreciative people, and their wonderful singing gave a real feel of fellowship – one or two tears were even noticed in the dancers also! The song – 'Jerusalem the Golden' – resounded through the whole building. I will also add that the hall in which we danced and our audience sang was named after the cousin of one of my dancers who I believe had been lost in the horrors of Auschwitz. I don't think I've ever experienced such wonderful togetherness before, and we afterwards received a really lovely letter of thanks and appreciation from the members of the synagogue. From memory (thirty-three years later) I think it was called the Malcolm Locker Hall. I still have all those letters! How glad I am that we brought a little lightness into their lives!

During my frequent visits to Hungary I added tremendously to my range of material.

Around 1985 Selpar had welcomed Anthea into our midst. As a musician and trained singer she immediately slotted in, despite having dreadful problems where she worked as a teacher and musician in a primary school in Birmingham. Over the years we got to know each other and (I know she would agree) the pastoral work I did at school helped her to accept help from me. She knew my wonderful mother for the short time that was left, and I hope she would say that I helped her somewhat when, later, her own mother died.

Marie left our house in 1988, shortly after Mum died – leaving for pastures new. We kept in contact for many years, but she died about two years ago in a rest home near to her sister in Ross.

Another bombshell fell when her sister told me Marie had changed her will so now only half of this house where I live is mine! And its condition must be kept up by me!

Back to school and the second dance-and-song drama which my mother had been able to come and see! Drawing on the work I absorbed – yes – in Hungary, this one in 1982 was based on an old man looking back on his childhood. Again, my mother's sketches were used for the programme and the cyclorama on the stage.

What is more, no recorded tapes were to be used; we had Mrs Lancett and her wonderful fingers on the grand piano in the school hall. With her knowledge and skill, and having heard so much of the music I always brought back with me, that lady could make a piano sound remarkably similar to a cimbalom (an instrument so frequently used by Gypsy and folk bands alike). She spent hours transcribing my tapes on to manuscript paper!

The old man (played by the head of English on the school staff) strolled on to the stage in full costume – black trousers tucked into (my) boots, full-sleeved white shirt, black waistcoat and a copy of a herdsman's coat (very decorated and authentic) over his shoulders. He was remembering his youth! Half leaning on his stick, he came to the front of the stage to sing a few verses of an old Hungarian song – in Hungarian!

In translation:

> I am going, I am going.
> Long the road I travel –
> Long and dusty roadside,
> Cloak of dust around me. . . .

It had three verses.

I had lent him a recording of the song, and he did really sound like a Hungarian elder. Mrs Lancett on the piano played at full

110

throttle. It was really wonderful, like a cimbalom brought to life!

Then came the children, singing and dancing at the same time. Then older children performed more-difficult dances, followed by a superb csardas (couple dance) while the old man nodded and sometimes clapped while sitting on a bench against a wall with (imitation) onions in strings and various-coloured peppers hanging there. Occasionally he thumped his stick in time to the music.

At the end of the many songs and dances, depicting some older couples, he wandered off and the team danced and sang at the front of the stage for the finale!

The audience was so happy, and loud in their praises. I addressed the front row of councillors and members of the education committee, pointing out – at a stage when peripatetic musicians working in schools were faced with redundancy – that our show could not have been produced without Mrs Lancett. We kept her for quite a long time – at least another term! Very opportunely, her daughter was one of the dancers!

I have to say that, very sadly, a few years later, just after my last visit to see her in a residential home, cared for by others, she died. But now there should be a lovely rose bush in the home's garden, planted there at my request by another resident.

CHAPTER XVI

FURTHER TRAVELS

The first time I flew to Hungary I found I was sitting beside Ashley. He was off to language school at Debrecen University; I was off to dance school in Vác. Because it was not the first time for him, he talked quite freely of how his course was led. We agreed that on returning to England we would meet up at the hotel in Birmingham where he was the manager. He invited me, with other people from the Midlands who had been on his course, to an evening swapping experiences in his comfortable flat in the hotel. Of course, he had had to learn a lot of skills as he made his way upwards in his chosen career as a manager, and he was an excellent chef as well as being fully trained in hospitality skills. We enjoyed an excellent Hungarian meal and a fun evening.

Later on, over the next few years or so, we quite by accident seemed to meet at Heathrow again and again. We both spoke of our various experiences, and I realised that he was as committed to Hungary as I was.

Visiting me at home one day, he spoke of his hopes and dreams – mainly to be a guide for groups visiting Hungary. In a nutshell, he wanted to show other people how he had fallen in love with that lovely little country. That is what he has gone on to do, and now I believe he has a home there.

A few years after our first meeting at the airport, he phoned me to invite me to dinner at the Buttery Bar of the hotel.

As soon as we'd settled he said, "You know, when you attend a summer course in Hungary, they automatically send application forms for the next year's course!"

He went up to fetch them and discovered he'd been sent a duplicate set of papers as well! He always made sure that any hotel he worked in had a good stock of excellent Hungarian wines, and with our first bottle and a good steak we discussed the information required on these forms. By the end of the meal – and quite a lot of wine – having for fun filled in all necessary answers, I left to go home.

About three days later, Ashley phoned me at work to ask, "Do you remember the forms we filled in last week?"

I was puzzled. "No," I hesitantly replied.

"Well, I've posted them!" came the response.

About three weeks later I phoned Ashley to ask what a letter I'd received (in Hungarian, of course) was all about.

"Oh, good – you're accepted. We'll go together!"

I came out of the staffroom phone cupboard laughing my head off.

So, off to college again, to learn Hungarian! We were in different classes – he for the more fluent students, my class was for the beginners. I did make a little progress, but it was hard work. To this day my Hungarian speech is really limited to being polite (greetings, etc.), reading a menu and asking for what I'd like, such as a specific shop or bus stop, etc.

Magda, puzzled at my learning the language, said it wasn't really necessary as I had some German anyway, but I felt that at least I should know how to greet her neighbours, etc.

The weekends were free, so Ashley and I booked simple accommodation from Debrecen and he showed me parts of the country – mostly in the east – that I had not yet visited. I was fairly familiar, by Magda taking me, with some lovely scenic areas and well-known traditional towns and villages.

In my class I met mostly Scandinavians and one Canadian as our class was taught through English. We had fun excursions to the market and enjoyed being together.

My accommodation was another matter. I shared a room with two young women from a country I'd visited twice, but they were not so comfortable with me. The older (and much bigger) one generally ignored me and used up all the hot water in the shower! When I was asked if in my travels – twice – to her country I had visited the capital city, I honestly said I hadn't. I think that was her problem, though in another visit I put that right. When they returned from a group visit to Budapest, the younger woman was full of praise – the shops, the availability of lovely items, the wonderful buildings! Her companion was rather sour about it.

A Finnish girl and I kept in contact even after the course was finished. A lot of her class time was spent making sketches – each time she pushed her notebook over to show me Winnie the Pooh in various poses. She was studying the language as a requirement for a librarian course, which she hoped might gain her more promotion. For her thesis she asked me for bear pictures to use, and when I got home my mother painted a lovely picture of one for her. After her thesis was approved, it was framed for her bedroom wall. A lovely thing to remember!

We were taken out as a group to interesting places, such as the Great Market, which was so very interesting. One man in our group – a Canadian who professionally was a photographer and who always had at least two cameras with him – gave me a lovely gift, which I still have, of a solid-silver American dollar. It was a lovely touch, I thought, as he acknowledged my interest in Hungary – and by then quite a lot of knowledge of the Hungarian way of life.

In the early days of taking ski parties to Europe from Yardley Grammar School, one evening after a shopping trip – Salzburg, was it? I can't remember – as we assembled for dinner that evening one of the older boys told me that in passing he had noticed my bedroom door was slightly open. He and another accompanied me, and as I pushed the door open to see into the room a large flash exploded – a third boy had taken a lovely photo of my response to seeing my bed bedecked with some really lovely gifts. There was a woven runner, a finely carved wooden plate, and a group of six glasses, unmistakably for schnapps (about two and a half inches high), each one nestling in a lovely leather cup. What an experience and what a lovely way of saying thank you for the trip and all it entailed! They were aware of my fondness for local crafts.

One day I received a letter from one of a group of boys who had worked very hard to perfect their high level of couple and men's Hungarian dances. They were all by now at university.

"Please will you do a students' reunion instead of a school ski trip this next season?"

What an opportunity that was! They had skied before, with Yardley pupils.

The first problem was voiced when we met up at The Swan, Yardley, for our coach to Heathrow. One lad, Douglas, hadn't renewed his passport – he had assumed that the previous one was OK. Oh dear, it was out of date!

"Well, you can take a chance, but it's going to be very tricky, or you can forgo the trip."

He took the chance!

Leaving England, the situation was frowned at, but they let him through on our side of the Channel! Arriving in Munich they smiled and let him through. A coach was waiting for us.

We had excellent conditions for the skiing and other activities in Austria that year.

One day Douglas came to say he'd timed a current pop song that the DJ in the bar had, and the rhythms and phrases (he was a very competent musician) were just right for one of their men's dances – a verbunk (soldiers' recruiting dance). Could they dance it in the bar? They did, and so very well that they had to give encore after encore. I will admit that I, in a suitable dress and high-heeled shoes and sitting right in front of them, had my feet tapping away to keep them going, phrase by phrase, quite professionally!

When the day of departure came, we were told that because of dense fog the airport was closed down and we were to enjoy an extra day and night. The next day was another difficult one as regards the passport. I went through the barrier, passport checked, and stayed close. The others moved up so that Douglas was next!

For the rest of my life I will hear the border policeman saying, "That ist not gutt!"

I faced him and, indicating my student, said in German, "He came in with us and he goes out with us!" All the time I was hand-waving to make my point.

Well, after quite a lot of spitting out "Ist not gutt!" Douglas was allowed through; so, very relieved, we went out to board the plane. We weren't leaving from Munich (where we landed), but from Nuremberg, as Munich was not only 'fogged in', but teeming with other school parties.

And so the event was over. I was terribly sorry to hear some years ago that Douglas had died. He had been to see me once or twice, and on one occasion I went to where he was living and we had lunch together in the local pub.

I was asked one year if I had any senior girl in the dance group who would be happy to apply for a bursary being awarded through the generosity of the Jewish community in Solihull, of which the current mayor, Mrs Hall, was a member. Joy – a beautiful dancer – jumped at the chance. It was an opportunity to travel throughout Israel and, through enquiry and discovery, find information pertaining to her chosen career within the medical field. There would be a boy (from another school) and herself chosen that year. After some very exhausting meetings with the committee, and after many moments seeking advice from me – regarding her appearance and dress for each occasion – the final meeting was to be attended by the Chief Rabbi, who was coming up from London for the occasion. At that final meeting I had to advise her to tell them that, unknown to her, her parents had set aside that summer to take her for the first time to meet her family in Nigeria – family she had never met before.

"What should I do?" was her question for me.

I answered, "Be honest from the very first and explain what has happened."

They were so impressed that they granted her the bursary, but held it over for a year. One condition was that she, on her return, would address the Jewish congregation to describe her experiences in Israel.

After her return she related how while staying with groups of students who always seemed to have music on she actually taught them some of their own traditional folk dances! She did so well and discovered such a lot. The other students appreciated the fact that Israeli dance had come from Tel Aviv to Swansea, then on to Yardley Grammar School and ultimately back to Israel! I was so glad!

The last time I saw her was after her return home from Israel, when she entered the large hall and approached the committee. She was dressed in the full costume of a woman from Nigeria – a full-length dress of cream fabric decorated with the most lovely purple print of tropical plants and a matching headdress in the same cloth tied in the traditional manner with sharp 'points' – a regal figure indeed. Her parents followed, approaching the committee to give thanks. I still don't know who was the proudest – she herself, her parents or her school!

In Hungary the teaching of music is most important, as I have been lucky enough to witness. All classes are taught through what is known as the Kodály System, and I have twice been asked to sit in on a session by a teacher I met at my first dance course in Vác and later in some of the many classes Magda taught.

On my first visit to Vác I took my guitar – by then a reputable one with a lovely tone, which I often played for myself.

One day in the lunch break I was asked to play and sing a traditional song; and knowing the Hungarians' love of history, I chose 'Greensleeves'. They were quite excited at the thought that it has been attributed to Henry VIII! The Tudor period was very graceful in its music and art, and of course its dress, and this little song has always been a favourite of mine because I can almost visualise the Tudor setting.

I was absolutely astounded when I realised that all the class, sitting on gym benches in front of me, were actually writing down the notation of the melody itself. I played it once, then involved

Zoli Bácsi, the pianist, for the final phrase – with a change of key for the last chord from E minor to E major, which makes quite a difference. Then I had to play it and sing it again so that they could check their notes!

Bringing my guitar home, though, was quite a problem. It was in its canvas case, which was regarded with great suspicion. The outside pocket was scrabbled through, and all the sheet music was tipped out. I had nothing to declare, and I got very cross, indicating, by pointing, that my guitar came in with me and my guitar would go out with me! I learnt then that I should have got a stamped permit on entry. Ah well – a lesson learnt.

When Magda's husband was ill in hospital, I went with her to visit him. He and his family were, and still are, very close to me. However, when the inevitable happened and he died, Magda phoned to tell me, giving also the date and time of the funeral. Five minutes later I was criticising myself for not suggesting I attend the funeral.

I phoned to ask her, "Would you like me to come?"

A lady of few words, all she said was "Yes, please!" and I was quickly preparing for the journey.

On arrival at Budapest Airport, I had to join a long line of businessmen – there for a conference.

I muttered, "I hope this doesn't take too long – I've got a funeral to attend."

Immediately, the chap in front called up the line, "Let this lady through. She's got a funeral to get to."

As one, they moved to let me through!

The taxi driver was very kind too. When he was given the address I wanted to reach, and that of the church also, "We get to the house!" was his response.

I was slightly later than I'd hoped, but the whole family had patiently waited for me.

The service was beautiful. I met and was greeted by many people I had met through dance, etc., and afterwards, back at Magda's apartment, I was quite undone when the toast 'to a friend who has come so far' was made by her eldest son. I stayed for a few days to keep Magda company for a while before returning home. The details of that occasion are still very vivid in my mind. There's no doubt I was part of the family.

When Magda came (about four or five times) to our SIFD summer school, I always asked Jack, the organiser, to extend her dates for the visa, which enabled her to spend a little holiday time with me. One year her husband also came, and on a very wet and stormy day I took them up to Cheshire for lunch with my mother. Dad had died in 1976 and they were all so glad to meet. It was a lovely day for us all.

In 1988, after my mother's death, I was summoned by phone: "Sybil, it's time you came to me."

Within a few hours I was packed and ready to go. I could not possibly have refused, and it was a wonderful comfort to be with Magda, who by now, I realised, was a surrogate mother to me. That was where I was *meant* to be, under the circumstances, and I am forever grateful for her kindness, thoughtfulness and love.

When Magda died, some years later, I was unable to go to her funeral, but even at a distance I felt close to them all. It seems that sundry surgical procedures have often got in the way of events I wished to attend.

Twice in recent years, Anthea and I have made the journey to Budapest with the travel agency for which Ashley and now some of his family are guides. I know that when taking city tours for holidaymakers he will probably read my poem 'A Magyarazat' to the travellers, as he did when we were there with them. On each of those visits we have been lucky to spend an evening catching up with Magda's daughter Kati. We still continue to connect, and Kati is, as her mother was, always concerned for my welfare. It makes me feel very humble that her caring reaches so far across from Hungary to England, and it is a friendship we both value.

CHAPTER XVII

TEACHING MUSIC

In my last year at Yardley (1985–6), before taking early retirement, I was summoned to the headmaster's office.

"Sybil, I want you to take music with all the third-year classes [there were six of them] and 2Y in the other block."

Our music studio was situated on the top floor, above a staff workroom where, apparently, little was done in what time staff had to spend there – preparing, or marking books before their next class. The atmosphere was not conducive to concentration!

We argued over my ability, and each point I raised was opposed. I had had a mere six months of learning to play the piano when I was thirteen, before we moved from the north-east to Cheshire on account of my father's job.

At Yardley I had built up a small lunchtime group – I would play guitar for them while they sang, and we had performed in church one year for our Christmas service.

When I mentioned not even knowing what the syllabus should be, "Write your own and I'll OK it!" was his answer.

"It's not feasible – I wasn't even taught music myself!"

"I've heard you teaching music through dance!"

So it went on, and at the end of the day I came home very, very worried.

Sitting in the lounge, I looked about me. 'Those may do the trick!' I thought, looking at the far wall, on which hung three beautiful folk instruments: a balalaika (Russian), a cimbalom (Romanian) and a cittera (Hungarian). See photos.

I do hope, in my reflective moments, that other colleagues, other teachers, other individuals who are ever pushed (I hesitate to use the word 'bullied') into suddenly changing their programme can be relieved of one major concern – will the kids know what's happening?

That day I was given no choice but to follow instructions and dip into a subject which, although I love it in my life, I had no real experience of teaching. I could only do some deep thinking – some thoughtful preparation – and hope for the best!

At the end of lunchtime, when I was doing my best to stay positive, yet at the same time almost reduced to the level of a student on teaching practice, there was a gentle tap on my door.

"Come in."

And there was Ronnie, a member of the class for which I was preparing myself.

"Hello, Miss. I've heard you're taking us for music – is there anything I could carry for you?"

That small, very polite thirteen-year-old seemed to open a curtain for me. His was not a 'difficult' class, but the subject . . . ? Politeness, concern and even a tone of caring were all in his attitude. This small lad, obviously brought up to face his 'superiors' with respect, has left an indelible impression with me!

I do hope that, as the only pupil in three years to opt for music within his GCSE courses, he has managed to be successful. I handed him my balalaika, and I remember his approach and – yes – his caring attitude, his concern and trust as he took the instrument with care. As I opened all the doors we needed to pass through, I thought I'd never met such reverence for an item in a thirteen-year-old boy – unless the item was his!

When the boys and girls were sitting down and Ronnie had so carefully put the instrument on the table, the questions started. Ultimately, after explaining how, when and from where it had come, we started the lesson. I played a very simple little tune (the first line of a tune yet to come), and Ronnie's job was to repeat it. As the balalaika is a fretted instrument that wasn't so difficult! The class were so intrigued, and they gave him a gentle clap. Then Ronnie had to take the instrument to a vacant desk at the back of the room, call out a friend and teach him how to play the little melody. Then, if he was satisfied, he had to return to his own place while the boy or girl called out a third child to show him or her. It took at least two whole sessions for them all to try it out. It seemed to spark their curiosity, but it was up to me to ignite a flame. Leaving the room later, they went downstairs, most of them gently humming the first phrase of 'The Birch Tree'.

My plan included playing an LP with a splendid picture on the cover of the Ossipov Balalaika Orchestra, showing the range of the instruments from small to huge (double-bass-sized).

With the words on the blackboard and the right track playing, they gently sang the folk song right through. So now my planned programme had started. They learnt about Tchaikovsky's Group of Five, learnt about the social changes in Russia, listened to a recording of the composer's Fourth Symphony in F and raised a hand each time they heard even an echo of the song they had learnt, which appears in the symphony's last movement!

There was no doubt about it – they hadn't, apparently, been bored. My certainty that it takes just a spark to ignite a flame had paid off.

After a few lessons, we moved on, this time by way of my lovely cimbalom, so loved by Gypsies and folk groups alike. The hammers for it I had brought back from a music shop in Budapest. It is similar to an English hammer dulcimer, but oh, so much more melodious! Often the hammer dulcimer is seen and heard, but the effect is much more clickety-clackety. Perhaps it is more suited to English folk dance and clog dancing.

Cimbaloms are frequently found in Hungary and Romania, but this one is extra-special. It was made for me by a most interesting craftsman, and his wife added the decoration and fretwork. He even managed to seek out John Leech – at that time the best player of the instrument in England – to check its tuning and other fine points. His work with instruments came about when he was a large-truck driver, frequently travelling to Amsterdam. In the intervals between unloading and reloading for the return voyage, he spent a lot of time in museums and art galleries, where he became intrigued by the many instruments in the paintings of Old Masters. He set up his workshop on a farm, using different outbuildings for different parts of the process, such as glueing, varnishing and sanding, to name but a few of them.

When I heard about him, I suggested that some of the Selpar dance group should pay him a visit (prearranged). When we arrived we were so surprised to see the vast range of instruments he could show us. Rod Perkins bought, there and then, a hurdy-gurdy – an instrument with keys, very popular in France, I believe. Having tried out the cimbalom, playing a favourite slow csardas of Hungary, he took details for my order and asked me to send him a copy of the very melodious tune I had played!

Then, ultimately, it was taken into class – something I'd never expected to happen. I showed the class a picture of the cimbalom being played, and gave a short geographical description of Romania and the Danube as an introduction to Enescu's 'First Romanian Rhapsody'. Enescu is rarely heard in this country, sadly, but his two rhapsodies are well worth listening to. In the case of my class, they mentally saw in the music the beautiful Danube area in all its glory. I pointed out, with a chalk line, the river flowing from Central Germany along the northern border to the Danube Bend, then southwards into Hungary, later to be joined by the Tisza river. Changes occurred in the pace of the music as we were rushed through the Iron Gates (a geological feature), the river following an ever widening path until it divides many times before reaching the coast of the Black Sea. It is a most dramatic 'vision of sound'. The calm of the river is depicted where its many outlets form the estuary, a place where many members of the RSPB and other groups pay summer visits to seek out the different species amongst the rushes and the reeds. It needs to be seen to be believed!

To judge from the children's comments, most, if not all, of these thirteen-year-old boys and girls thoroughly enjoyed the 'story and pictures in sound' of Enescu's 'First Romanian Rhapsody'.

Then came the cittera (Hungarian zither), another fretted string instrument. This instrument also was specially made for me in Hungary, where a craftsman has to have reached the level of master craftsman to sell it.

While attending one of my numerous dance workshops, there was an opportunity to take part in this area of folk tradition. When asked if I would like to join in, of course I expressed my thanks. After a few evenings with the teacher, I was asked if, for collection at my next visit, I would like one to be made for me. Yes! I was asked if I wished the instrument to be decorated or plain, and I opted for plain as it might, someday, be taken into school. (Little did I know then!)

This instrument is often played by musicians old and young, near to or even outside cafés. I've seen them balanced across knees, or even on a wall, and the sound is really very lovely – but also somewhat intriguing.

However, when the time came for me to collect it I saw the craftsman had decorated it with small coloured flowers, a bird and other natural reminders of the countryside.

With this instrument we compare the works of Kodály (Kodai) or Bartók in Hungary with the works of Cecil Sharp, an Englishman. Through their diligent searches for original songs and dances in their respective countries, an amazing collection of English and Hungarian traditional music is still available today. They all included, when writing symphonies or rhapsodies, musical phrases or other reminders of their roots. In Kodály's case, many of the Hungarian dance tunes, particularly for girls, can be heard both in recordings and in their *Tanz Ház* (folk-dance clubs) by those of us who are interested in their traditional dances.

When I commented on the cittera's decoration, I was told, "He would make it quite beautiful because it was going out of the country." A very moving reply!

Having taken a morning assembly on one occasion, I had to improvise a lesson in a classroom. No piano, no recording equipment – just me, with a classroom on each side of us! I didn't even have my guitar with me. This was a class of thirteen-year-olds – middle-school pupils. In the assembly I had pointed out various arguments and squabbles – if not fights – both in the building and in the playground, so harmony was very much in my mind that day.

The class was split into four groups – one in each quarter of the room. Boys with broken voices were near the door, those not yet changed in the opposite corner. Likewise the girls: those with clear, high voices (but no screaming) and those with richer voices (but no shouting) were in the two remaining quarters of the room.

I stood centrally. Dare I? Should I risk it? Long pause for thought! Get on and do it!

In turn, each group was to copy my hum. To each corner in turn I gave a note: C for the first group of boys, E for the second group of boys, G for the first group of girls and the higher C for the last group. Brilliant! They were keen for more. I taught breathing techniques (no lifted shoulders, but use of the diaphragm, etc.). We tried combinations of thirds, as by now there was a stave drawn on the board with these four notes marked. Then the big build-up – C-E-G-C on the board – giving me time to repeat each note singly. Then I raised both hands and we had the perfect chord as they all combined!

They were involved, amazed and even elated, and so was I. One boy leant forward in his group and called out, "Was that us?" It really was a beautiful sound, and I made the comment that real harmony is worth hearing. They obviously were happy, and I was absolutely over the moon.

Thank you, Mr Lavery. I think we both had some surprises there!

This class, 2Y, was in the Formans Road building, and had already been roped in by their teacher when young voices were taught a few European folk songs to sing from the platform steps during one of our dance events.

When I arrived, guitar in hand, they were all very welcoming and bright-eyed for their new teacher. Of course, they wanted me to play my guitar, so for starters I gave them the words for 'The Happy Wanderer', which they sang well and happily as I played.

Then it was time to talk rhythm – both on-beat and offbeat – to help them with the songs they were to sing during the performances.

The next item was to be percussion, and they were given very basic notes about sound. I suggested they made, at home, some quite basic drums and rattles, and also experimented with strips very tightly attached at each end which would ping when plucked. Blowing across bottles containing different depths of water also appealed.

We had no record player or other means for me to give them sounds as played by professional musicians, but simple songs with guitar backing allowed them a chance to tap, bang or shake whatever they had brought to school.

Following their (at home) experiments with pop bottles, etc., quite a few children, with surprising patience, actually produced some good sounds. This next item proved the most engaging for them – I showed the class the cover of an LP by George Zamfir, a panpipes expert, and I described how the instrument was played, throwing in a little science regarding longer pipes producing deeper sounds, etc. Quite a few of them had discovered a similar effect when experimenting with different depths of liquid in equally sized bottles.

Then our time was over for that taster of the work I'd initially been so doubtful about.

One week later, as I walked across the hall to 2Y's classroom, the unmistakable sound of pan pipes reached me! When I opened the door all the boys and girls (eleven to twelve years old) looked a little worried.

"Who was playing pan pipes?"

"I was, Miss," a very small boy replied, looking rather sheepish, but my broad grin put his worries to rest. "I didn't make 'em, Miss!"

"Who did? I think it's like seeing a miracle," I said.

"I made them," said Richard, a taller boy than the player.

My enthusiasm knew no bounds, even though the little tune did resemble 'Baa Baa Black Sheep'. Richard explained that his father helped by getting un-notched bamboo canes from a garden centre. Then, between them, they had cleaned out the centres leaving a smooth surface!

The wrapping of the cross-sticks holding all the pipes together was made from fine-linen string. Then the lower ends were sealed with Plasticine. The likeness to the original in the picture Richard had seen was unbelievable. All the children were delighted for Richard's sake.

At half-term I asked him if I could borrow the set of eight pipes (all, at that time, tuned to a clear octave of eight notes). Yes, he said when I explained I'd be going to see friends in Hungary and I wanted them to see what can happen in an English school. On my return, I gave Richard back his panpipes and told him that my friends were amazed.

Some weeks later I retired, and, before I left, Richard came to tell me he would like to give me his instrument. It was very difficult to hide a tear or two as I thanked him.

See photos of instruments.

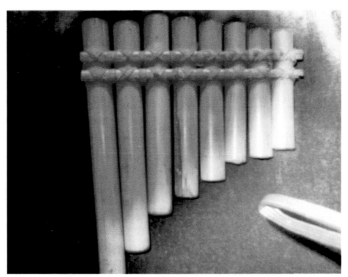

Richard's pan pipes – made as his homework.

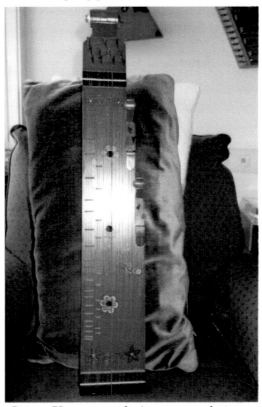

Cittera (Hungarian zither), pronounced tsittera.

Cimbalom (Hungarian dulcimer), pronounced tsimbalom.

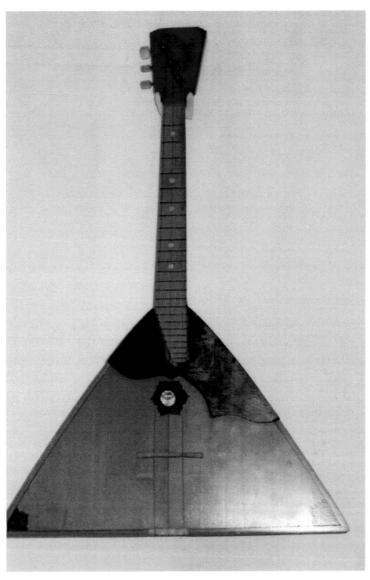

Balalaika from Russia.

CHAPTER XVIII

THE DAY OF THE FIRE!

I arrived at school one morning to find that sometime during the previous evening some thoughtless idiots had apparently set fire to a refuse bin containing fish-and-chip papers and hurled it through the window of the gym storeroom, which not only led into the gym, but was directly beneath my small changing room/ office!

Chris Watts, the boys' PE master, was as furious as I was. The vaulting apparatus and all the landing mats, etc., were ruined; nearby fixtures in the gym were now unusable.

I insisted, as a means of speeding up the reparation work, that a member of the education committee should be called in to see the damage.

The floor in my little room above had become dangerously 'raised' because of the heat, but fortunately my records – paper or musical – were not damaged. Also, Mrs Watts (history) found the toilet unusable as the whole thing was split asunder.

A member of the education committee arrived, and with me watched some of the PE activity in the assembly hall.

I was shocked and angry when this person, both taller and broader than I, simply said, "And if you think that we will give you a grant for any more trips to Hungary, you can think again – in fact you can expect to find your position in danger!"

My reply was "And if you think that research and learning – whatever the topic – is dependant on your paltry grant, I'm afraid *you* will have to think again. Are you trying to tell me that research and learning are ever finished? Is there an end to research? The small grant would never even cover the cost of all the necessary items I brought home – books, reams of notes, photographs, even pieces of costume – all these items to be used educationally in school."

Twice I had been given leave of absence to attend special events – workshops mostly, but also international festivals of folk culture in various parts of Hungary. What is more, that aspect of my teaching career already stretched beyond Yardley and was helped along by teachers I had met while researching. Yes, it was pleasant, but I can assure you that it was no holiday! While I had some help in attending workshops, at least twice a year they took place during school holidays. If I was away at any time, I was either skiing, teaching youngsters to enjoy the sport or – yes – dancing!

CHAPTER XIX

THE PETO INSTITUTE

Between 1968 and the end of the century, I was in and out of Hungary two, three or even four times a year to attend workshops, but I occasionally managed a little taste of a holiday. On one occasion I stayed at the apartment of a family I met originally in the UK. I had given space to a scientist who was involved in research work at Birmingham University. Her husband worked there also for a time and their daughter was born in Birmingham. Their house at that time was in Oroshaza, not too far from Debrecen, in the east of Hungary, where I studied the language.

She was first introduced to me by a member of Selpar, who worked in the same department at the university. When she joined Selpar she was so pleased to see Hungarian dancing as taught in Hungary when she was a girl in school. Her work lasted for some time, and occasionally I had all three of them staying with me. Judit's father had moved to Pécs, in the west of Hungary, and we went there by car – a long, long, hot journey. Juditka (their daughter) and I amused ourselves by spotting the nests of cranes (the bird variety!), which nested seemingly unconcerned on the very tops of telegraph/power poles!

From there (near the Croatian border) we spent the day in the Baranya region. We drove through a small settlement with single-storey houses on one side and a line of bodegas opposite – the red wines of this area are good.

Since then my friends have settled there, where Judit (the

mother) now holds a prestigious position in the University of Pécs – pronounced Paych.

As head of middle school, I was available for any parents who wished, or needed, to see me. One afternoon, the father of one of the girls came to see me. Having discussed his daughter's achievements, etc., he referred to a book on my desk – *Learn Hungarian* – and described the system of the Peto Institute for Conductive Education, which was just being set up in Birmingham. One could describe the system as a method of helping to improve the lives and abilities of children who suffer, through no fault of their own, with mental or physical disabilities – socialising them, improving their movement and strength control, increasing their skill levels towards a more fulfilling future. I accepted his invitation to visit the children one afternoon when they were meeting in a building in Northfield, in outer Birmingham.

I dressed carefully in a very colourful Hungarian costume and took with me some recordings of children's folk dances. I was greeted by the children with much joy and smiles and laughter. We all assembled in a circle, at first, to try out some very simple steps to the music, then transferred the steps into partnered pairs – making, breaking and remaking the circle. They were so happy.

Many had mobility problems, but they could all smile throughout these little exercises. Then we had a pause and I had a cup of tea! Sitting amongst them, I received so many hugs and whispered 'secrets' that I, too, enjoyed myself. The approach and attitude of the teachers was a lesson in itself in love and care for the improvement in each child's welfare and possible future.

When I left them – giving a final twirl of my petticoats – they were all smiling, and as a gift I was given a stand bearing a model of a pair of silver special-needs boots. They are on a shelf where I see them each time I go upstairs – a lovely gift reserved for positive-thinking visitors.

I heard that the group moved to different accommodation (like me), but I know the work goes on!

CHAPTER XX

INVOLVING THE BOYS!

Occasionally some boys came to try out a bit of folk dance. Two from year 2 ended up by taking part in one of the two Folk Dance and Song productions put on stage. The first one was the old lady's reminiscence of her wedding. The second one depicted an old man looking back towards his own youth in the village.

At Yardley there had frequently been occasions when upper-fifth or sixth-form boys and girls met their ultimate 'mate'. Some of these girls were in the senior dance group. Ultimately, their boyfriends came to join in – rainy lunch hours saw many a young man – and a member of staff – trying hard to reproduce the very well-known (in Hungary) men's dances and soldiers' recruiting dances dating back to the Austro-Hungarian Empire, when the Emperor sent out good male dancers in uniform to entice the country lads into the army! Strength and stamina they certainly had, and I was qualified to teach them!

There was an occasion when the boys' group danced for the twenty-first birthday of one of them (Douglas), and this involved my taking with me their Hungarian boots and joining them in the toilet area to rehearse the dances! They also rehearsed a couples dance with me.

On one ski trip this same group of boys – now all university students – put on a demonstration with the backing of the DJ in the bar. Very successful! Many encores were called for!

The senior girls' group was very popular with elderly people who spent some days in their local Day Centre. The elderly folk were so happy to have us, and occasionally they would offer me an item of clothing or even a gramophone record applicable to what we did, to help with our wardrobe, etc. These outings resulted in memories to be kept!

As I mentioned earlier, I usually drove the school minibus and the overflow were taken in a car driven by Mrs Oxenbury – the mother of one of the girls, Susan, which was a great help. I heard recently that, sadly, she had died of the same illness as my sister Helen; and although I haven't been able to trace Susan, if she reads this she will know how much I appreciated her mother's help and how sorry I am to hear that she's lost her mother – a stalwart helper whenever I needed her. A photo of Susan – and others – dancing stands in a cabinet in my dining room.

Apart from finally getting to enjoy MED from Canley, the topic actually came to my rescue on one or two occasions. This I was reminded of today when reading the list of Britain's best loved classical pieces of music. Number five on the list is Vaughan Williams' 'Fantasia on a Theme by Thomas Tallis'. For some reason this music inspired images all around me as I drove to school one day. In my mind's eye I saw a tall turreted chateau, with huge trees in the estate around it, and mist rising from a stream where cattle were standing, wreathed in fine clouds of breath. All this was emphasised by diagonals of light streaming through the whole picture as the sun rose higher.

When I arrived at the school, I was given a message that my young assistant PE teacher would not be in that day. Oh dear! A quick check of both our timetables showed me that I was available to take her first- and second-year classes. What could I do? A record of the Vaughan Williams music I've mentioned was facing me from the top of the bookcase in my small room! Yes! That should do it. So I set up the record player on the edge of the platform, for the lesson was to be in the hall.

When the class was gathered, I gave them a verbal description of all that I'd imagined on my way that morning to school. They listened intently (for once) to the music, then separated into four groups quietly, but with a few hints given, and between them they created a lovely tableau of two magnificent pillared and arched buildings through which light was continually passing. It almost seemed to me as though they had (at eleven-plus years) produced a replica of the Parthenon (in Athens), and the final sequence was really beautiful. They loved gliding and moving throughout, so there were the movements of the gentle rays and the strength of the vertical pillars. Their imaginations created a lovely picture. This was yet another proof that youngsters can really be creative. We all enjoyed the lesson, and the girls (some of them) very successfully let their imaginations do the rest. It seemed to me then that Canley had proved to be enjoyable and useful – I enjoyed it too!

CHAPTER XXI

ACHIEVING YOUR GOAL

In Hungary, various trades owned holiday accommodation for their workforces. There, as union members, they could have a comparatively reasonably priced holiday. When my friends caught up with me and met me at Lake Balaton one summer in the 1970s, we – two grandparents, one granddaughter and their friend (me) – went to the hotel. I already had a good B & B accommodation, but because I could show my NUT card to the manager at the hotel I was able to take lunch and evening dinner with my friends.

Two events spring to mind. Often when I was out in the mountains on a skiing holiday I had a mouth organ in my pocket, and when I paused for a rest or to take a photo I'd give myself a tune, then proceed on my way. At Balaton one day, when walking by the lake with my family of three, I took the little mouth organ out and played a children's song, which Andrea (about eight years old) started skipping along to. It was a very happy suggestion from Magda and Endré (*Oma* and *Opa*, or Grandma and Grandpa), and another occasion that drew me even closer to the family.

One evening, towards the end of dinner, the big television in the dining room came on with its mighty message for the children present. We saw Máckö – Winnie the Pooh to me; Máckö (Teddy Bear) to all the children present – looking around the room (from the screen) then climbing stairs, changing into pyjamas, brushing his teeth, etc. Then he waved towards his audience, calling

"Goodnight, children" and disappearing. At that moment all the children left their tables and trotted happily up the stairs to bed. No complaints, no unhappy children – all of them doing just what the bear had told them to do! I'm smiling as I write this!

In many schools, and indeed many countries, I have found, they often say you teach the child first, but elsewhere the subject takes priority. I have used both approaches, but – believe me – the former, with the emphasis on the child, produces greater results. One tiny spark becomes a flame – even, perhaps, a furnace! Watch it develop!

One of my happiest surprises was to learn that the mother of one of my students wished her daughter to follow the path I had taken. Unfortunately, her application to a college to study PE in all its aspects was refused due to an apparent tendency to Raynaud's disease. This is a condition from which I have always suffered, but in her case there was the possibility of it reducing her ability to referee winter games and matches! I myself still suffer, due to an inherited poor circulatory system! It didn't stop me, though, and I feel she had a hurried and unfair assessment! She more than made up for it throughout her professional career and personal life. At times, when she applied for promotion in teaching posts, there were many hurdles to get over, but she did it. She trained fully as a teacher of primary schoolchildren, and then in the following years she qualified in the teaching of children with special educational needs. With those qualifications behind her, she found time (and energy) to gain a qualification in gymnastics – in order to be legally and professionally qualified to take classes after school where children could benefit from organised physical activities. How did she do it? Every single job application was a hurdle in front of her! She approached them all with the mental mantra we used in our dance group at school: "Nearly – a bit better – go on – faster – nearly OK – Yes!" She spent her latter years of teaching as headmistress of a primary school in a poor part of Liverpool.

I was like that all along – I believe that the child does and should come before all else.

139

During those years I was, sadly, unaware of her progression. Apparently, during a school reunion she told her friend, Sally Keepax, that she had wanted to contact me for ages.

I was sitting in my garden, recovering from surgery, when my neighbour summoned me to sign for a parcel delivery.

She asked me, "Who is it from?"

There was the card. I opened it and to this day, writing this page, there are tears.

> You changed my life.
> Thank you.
> You won't remember me, but I was José Davies. I am now José Reeves.
> With love,
> José. x

I phoned Sally to ask her to reach José, and she gave me her address. Then she phoned José to tell her the flowers had arrived. An hour later José phoned *me*! Then later she sent me a long letter of updates, including photos of her family. Like many Yardley Grammar School students, including Sally and Steve, she met her husband or wife while at school! A few weeks later there was delivered an enormous bottle of champagne – just in time for my birthday!

I only hope we can all meet up and reminisce.

Later I received a lovely card and photos that her husband had copied of the rehearsal for the dance-and-song wedding in which José was the bride. I am also shown – holding aloft a bottle (empty)! José is at my left shoulder!

Many of the costumes we used were made at home here – the wide-legged trousers and wide-sleeved shirts for the horsemen (cowboys of the great plain) in dark-blue or white cloth, the black trousers and waistcoats for other men, refashioned from suits bought from the school's second-hand shop, and the white shirts made from sheets supplied by friends.

Marie, who shared this house, was a highly qualified tailor and dressmaker, so there was help at hand. I bought a complete girl's

Kalocsa costume from a folk-craft shop in Budapest – this is the traditional dress of Kalocsa, a town on the Danube river south of Budapest. That town is famed for its decorative arts and crafts, and its traditional costumes are so colourful with flowered embroidery. The patterns are also used for the decoration of fine porcelain and can often be seen inside some of the old cottages, where the walls are totally covered by the work of painting women.

Kalocsa and Hollókö (further north) are both towns of special interest – I forget the proper titles. I know they have protected status.

My mother was a member of the North West Arts Committee, and a great friend of hers was Hungarian, so when it was announced that the national costume collection of Hungary was to be shown in a Manchester gallery I was, naturally, informed. I also had an invitation to the opening of this once-in-a-lifetime exhibition from the Hungarian ambassador. The whole exhibition was stopping over en route to a similar function in America.

So dressed to the nines, as they say, my friend in the Kalocsa costume and I in the costume of Galgamácsa took my mother to the opening. I had also been granted a photography permit for the following morning, before the exhibition was opened to the public. It was a wonderful evening – a most prestigious affair – and the Ambassador was very complimentary. My mother's friend, afterwards, took us to several of her Hungarian friends' homes where we were (dare I say 'of course'?) greeted traditionally with small glasses of tokay (wine). Then we went home to my mother's house in Sale. All along the very wide Washway Road (the road out to Chester) we had the company of a car which seemed to be playing games with us! Like the Wolverhampton road out of Birmingham, there are many, many traffic lights, and each time we stopped this other car was on our right. I remember there were two people and a little dog in that car. Eventually, although we were only going at about thirty-five miles per hour on a totally empty road, the police caught up with us. Oh dear! Rather than have them smell my breath (as driver) in my car, I got out of the car.

Now, Hungarian very fine-pleated skirts are not for sitting on! In restaurants, etc., the back of the skirt is often lifted over the back of the chair, so you sit on petticoats. I didn't drive wearing my skirt! I got quickly out of the car, and there I was, standing in my petticoats plus blouse, bodice, hat and boots, facing the police in full view!

Asked where we were going, I told them. Then they asked where we had been, and my eye caught an AA sign on a lamp post, to which I pointed. The sign read 'Hungarian Exhibition – Walker [I think] Gallery'. They did give me a ticket and the other car was well away! I think they were probably filling in a boring shift! At least it was a little unusual to find a driver half undressed! I paid the fine and said nothing about the hospitality visits.

CHAPTER XXII

MY FIRST HUNGARIAN COSTUME, BUT NOT MY LAST!

While staying in Vác with friends (also teachers) of my mentor, I was taken by car, driven by the daughter of the family there (like a somewhat thwarted Le Mans entry!), up into the hills to a little place called (I think) Vereségyháza – it's so long ago and tricky to remember. We drove fast up a very twisty road, passing on the way one or two (or more) people carrying what seem to be clothes of some sort! This trip was arranged as a surprise for me, and I wasn't told the destination. However, we reached a house that turned out to be that of the village schoolmaster, and word had been sent out that I was hoping to buy a local costume. Many young women had come to show me the choice available. The costumes are very much a part of their lives, and I felt so guilty that these pieces were being offered to me. They are very precious and come out for weddings, festivals, including church services such as Easter, and many other occasions. Boots I already had. The costume I chose here was being modelled by the daughter of my science-researcher friend, who later spent some months here in England with me. See photo.

The skirt (about five yards of it) was purple, finely pleated at the sides and back, with a brightly flowered inset apron as the front panel. The blouse was white with very full to-elbow sleeves. The bodice, like a small waistcoat, was white, embroidered all over with small flowers. It had a headdress/scarf in pink and a lovely shawl which crossed over at the front and was tied in a special way at the back. It had the most lovely broderie anglaise over most of it. That was the one I chose, and for it I paid a mere £15.

I didn't know then that it should not have been taken – as a piece of great value – out of the country; but as a great fuss was made at customs over my guitar, they missed the folk art, and I brought it home.

On another trip to Hungary I – on entry – got an OK for my guitar at customs (I'd learnt my lesson) and also a permit for my small tape recorder. I should have got my guitar OK'd on the previous trip! However, on examining the contents of my case when returning there again, the men were too preoccupied with showing each other my costume petticoats! I made sure of an OK for the costume as I might well be in need of it for bringing another one home as well!

Magda helped me to amass quite a collection over the years, and my lovely costumes were worn with great care and respect by members of Selpar, and of course the lovely dancing girls of Yardley Grammar School! Every trip I took saw me coming home with pairs of boots for both adults and school pupils.

On one memorable trip I brought back – with no problems – a shepherd's richly decorated felt coat, the cittera that was made specially for me, records, books and stacks of papers with all my notes on from my many workshop visits.

In Hungary every so often a major gathering used to happen. Young people whose parents had emigrated to the USA, Canada, etc., gathered in Budapest to learn, through lectures, sports and various visits, the traditions, language and culture of the land of their parents' birth.

CHAPTER XXIII

JUDIT

On one occasion I was asked to write out in English the notes and instructions for dances they were to be taught, and translations of poetry. All this I did with Magda's help and the use of cine film, etc. I was actually paid when I took these papers to the appropriate office in the city. I was paid £10 for the work, which had given me so much pleasure. Perhaps it was because of my very obvious love of the country that in 1978 I was offered the chance to live and work in Hungary. Because of my mother's health (Dad had already died) and the fact that I had a good job in the UK, I reluctantly had to turn it down.

Once, in Budapest, I was invited to a primary school. The teacher, Hasznosi Judit, I had met on my very first visit to Vác. (Note: In Hungary names are, to us, back to front.) Judit (pronounced Youdit) and I got on very well, and when she heard I was in Budapest on one occasion she invited me to 'observe' in her classes in a primary school. It seems that many teachers wear a white sleeved coat on top of their clothes – chalk in pocket, etc. Sensible! The lesson started by introducing this foreign teacher from England, and they all politely rose and wished me welcome – "*Yonapot kivanok*," if I remember rightly.

The lesson started with Kodály System hand and finger signs. Then, having been given a note, they followed Judit's hand signals and sang an octave. I was *most* impressed! Then they proceeded to follow, from their textbook, the notes of the song in front of them. Then we all clapped (gently) the rhythm and they sang the song (also gently) 'step-closing' with their feet. Amazing!

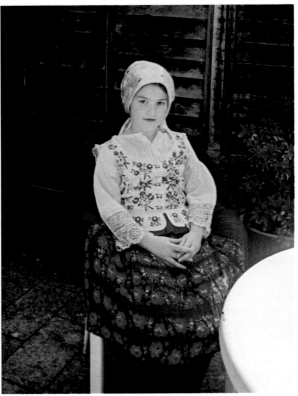

Juditka, daughter of my Hungarian guest, wearing my first original costume, bought in a small village north of Vàc, up in the hills.

A year or so later, I guided my friend Anthea with two other ladies from Selpar during a ten-day stay. Magda (my mentor) had arranged for us to use two apartments instead of a hotel. The residents were going on holiday, so we luxuriated, enjoying 'living Hungarian'. Mimi (Japanese) and Anne (French) were overjoyed with their visit, and as they were good churchgoers I took them to church for the 11-a.m. service on the Sunday. They were so overcome with the song which, as Anthea and I already knew, was sung by everyone at the end of the service.

Therefore while Anthea and I walked around the Bastion (the walls around the area, with lovely views down and around Castle Hill) they enjoyed a second church service!

Later that week, Hasznosi Judit invited us all to her school at the end of one day. She brought into the hall her school dance group. Those children were thrilled to give a demonstration to the teacher's friends, and they were very interested when she told them that I was a teacher of Hungarian dance.

At the end of their lovely little performance we (all four of us) were each presented with a bottle of Hungarian wine! It was such a lovely visit.

Each Christmas Judit sends me a DVD of the Christmas concert her choirs give in, I believe, the National Gallery. It's always very popular, apparently, and well attended.

Judit came to England one year, and having met her off the plane we were just in time to reach the Chateau Impney Hotel, here in Droitwich, for a lovely concert given (I believe) by some of the City of Birmingham Symphony Orchestra – a lovely occasion which we all, including my mother, enjoyed.

Judit came on Monday to my school, and visited our music department briefly, then joined me on the field where I was coaching various sporting and athletic events. That was something she hadn't experienced, and she took away some nice memories of our activities. We are still in contact.

CHAPTER XXIV

LESLIE HADDON

Some years after attaining his degree at Cambridge University, Leslie came to Birmingham University to study for his next qualification – his Masters degree.

In Cambridge he had joined in with a class taught by a Swiss colleague of mine in the SIFD. There he learnt more about Hungary and its dance traditions. When he came to the Midlands he was advised to find me and our by now established Selpar group.

He fitted in supremely well and was able to add a bit of his expertise to the fledgling group. Usually I partnered him for demonstrations/entertainments, etc., and as a good partner/example when I gave workshops to other branches of the SIFD. Even when he returned to London and married Sue, he would help out in an emergency.

The original teacher of the group in London, Alan, had sadly died and ultimately, on returning to London, Leslie took over the group there. He also, as I had hoped, followed my and Alan's pattern of 'going there and finding it' – travelling and joining in with native groups and clubs. Thank you, Leslie, very much for your contribution to what we both hold dear: original, traditional folk cultures and dance.

Another young man I met and taught in Selpar was Fred. . . . (See Chapter XXXII.)

Dancing with Leslie Haddon, Chamberlain Square, Birmingham, 1986.

CHAPTER XXV

MY TWO CATS

Some years ago, while the lounge was completely stripped of furniture for the decorator to work there, both Bartie (a large Tuxedo fellow) and Copper, a tortoiseshell with a little ginger hat, found me via the cat flap into the garage and another into the kitchen. Copper was a little cowed by her big friend and would jump off my lap if she heard him coming in! They both loved the one remaining chair (for a while under protective sheeting) with its velvety surface.

One day, on my return in the evening, having asked Simon to see they were out when he left, I was surprised to feel a furry presence against my leg as I filled the kettle in the kitchen. Copper it was – of course!

The next day, checking with Simon, he said that as I was renewing the carpet (I was giving it to him as he was doing up his own house, and as the underlay would also be changed) he'd taken pity on my waifs. There had been constant heavy downpourings all evening, so perhaps a 'little accident' wouldn't matter too much! I was very happy to know how well he'd looked after them!

They definitely needed a permanent home; but when the occasion arose when they needed veterinary treatment, I arranged with the owners that I would take them on as mine and register them with a local vet. Bartie loved freedom, but Copper was always a bit shy. When she crossed from the coffee table to reach my extended chair (feet up) she took quite a while to settle – an activity that attracted the attention of any friends I had with me.

Copper and me taking a rest!

Anthea and my Copper.

Copper enjoying the warmth of a hand-woven cushion.

Bartie – deep in 'cat dream', and my duvet!

She was usually settled by my singing quietly to her an old French song while my foot kept the rhythm of a foot on the pedal of a spinning wheel. This became her settling-down song. There were others, in German, Italian and even Hungarian, and if I paused there would be an enquiring lift of her head! I will confess now that sixteen years later, when I had no choice but to ask the vet to help her over the rainbow, I sang that same song to her – '*File la Laine*' ('Spin the Thread') – as she left me.

After a few years with me, one evening, as I opened a drawer for the next day's underwear, she jumped from the bed to the dressing table. The drawer had proved to be irresistible to her – in she popped and settled down. Then came Bartie, who did likewise. Not relishing the likelihood of furry undies, I put an old T-shirt in another drawer next to the first one, and Bartie *pushed* Copper into it. He, in the meantime, had been allocated a small hand towel in *his* drawer. I can only find one photo of them, but I remember clearly Bartie expressing the fact that he was the boss! Copper had the honour of having her photo taken on my bed, cuddled up beside one of the many bears in my collection! She was also shown one year in a copy of the Cats Protection magazine.

Sadly, Bartie succumbed to kidney failure, so the vet visited to take him to his rainbow. For days, Copper refused breakfast in their allotted space beside the kitchen table, but I had to set her place on the end of the table, so we breakfasted together!

Ultimately, she succumbed to an internal blockage – I think it was a nasty growth. So with tears and a heavy heart, she went, with me singing to her, to join Bartie.

A beautiful picture of her, beautifully crafted in felting, stands against my fireplace. It was crafted by the daughter of my home help, and it ultimately won first prize in a local arts-and-crafts competition. I know Copper watches me all the time. I do so miss her, but can't yet find my way to owning another cat. I do know that they had a far better life here with me, though!

CHAPTER XXVI

BACK TO WORK

Whenever I returned from a visit to Hungary with costumes, records, boots, etc., I was hardly home before jumping into my car and driving off to Nottingham, Swansea, Edinburgh or some other place where I had been pre-booked to tutor a workshop in Hungarian dance. Those were lovely, though quite exhausting visits, and I made a lot of friends right from my first acquaintance with the SIFD. After my second hip replacement I had to step back from the activity, but left the West Midlands group in the capable hands of Maggie Kaye.

One of my duties as head of middle school involved helping the third-year boys and girls choose their subjects for GCSE courses. This meant one or both parents and the boy or girl coming to my office to discuss the future of the youngster. This way, we could help them make an informed choice – usually with the agreement of subject teachers concerned. Then I had to deal with the paperwork, recording all the names and other information – lists and endless lists. The pastoral side of my position was at times quite distressing.

Some events occurred that can still upset me – events that don't stay in the office, but come home in one's heart and thoughts. My greatest regret, with the end of term looming and my expected emigration to Canada to fulfil the wishes of my Uncle George and become assistant manager of a beef station in Canada, was that I had to let go of two youngsters in particular – a boy and a girl, both from the same class. Their really major and very different problems I was instrumental in helping to put right. They were quite separate cases, but I think they both understood the position I was in. I was in no position to choose, and following a good leaving party at a country pub with my colleagues, including Susan (dancer) and her mother, they joined us for the great send-off and I received fantastic leaving gifts from them all.

Had I been able, through technology, to trace the progress of those two youngsters, I would not now be in a permanent state of regret regarding their progress – both work-wise and family-wise. If either of you read this, you will know that my circumstances at that time very much got in the way of what I've missed and would otherwise have done. It would not be either fair or responsible for me to say any more now, but I do remember you.

The bench in my garden was presented to me as a leaving gift. I still have it, and I see the school shield and motto ('Keep Troth') each time I am in the garden.

The weaver's storage rack crafted by one of my boys is very proudly used in my workroom, and, as mentioned before, I still have the panpipes Richard made and gave me when I retired. Until I was forced to stop weaving, due to a shoulder problem, I used the rack whenever I prepared a new shuttle. Now I can only look at it – but I remember the lad who made it, very frequently.

CHAPTER XXVII

ART AND MY MOTHER'S INFLUENCE

My mother had moved to her lovely bungalow in Droitwich in 1980. Her youngest brother, a high-powered businessman who was based in Tokyo, had asked me to look for a suitable property for her. My father had died in 1972. I looked for and found one about two miles from me, where she had a lovely garden with a spacious lounge opening on to it, a room for a studio and many helpful details she hadn't had previously.

Some years before she moved, through persuasion and an inner urge she had ventured far to give time and thought to painting. If I heard of a group going to Brussels, Rome, Nassau, Canada, etc., I made sure she went in company. On one memorable visit to Paris, she visited Picasso himself and spent a couple of days in his studio! Amsterdam (and the galleries there) was a huge draw for her and contrasted very much with Berdun, in the Spanish Pyrenees! Examples of her work are in many rooms here – each one a treasure.

Wherever she went she found herself painting for other people, and there are examples of her work still in the Bahamas, Tokyo and Canada. My own stairway is a gallery itself! She also, because of the depth of her knowledge and skills, completed restoration work for galleries and even antiques traders.

In 1982 we arranged a massive exhibition of her work here in Droitwich, which occupied the whole of the upper floor of the library. She, unlike many modern painters, could cover such a vast range of subjects, requiring an equally vast range of skills,

Mum, home from the annual academy exhibition opening.

One of my mother's lovely paintings. The view from the front window
– 52 Avonlea Road, Sale, Cheshire.

which she had developed in her younger days at college and with the best of tutors. Therefore we had to set up screens judiciously to separate, for example, life (the nude form) from 'costume' (portraits), etc. While my friend Marie served the visitors a glass of good white wine, I sat in a corner gently playing my guitar, and providing 'Sold' stickers for many of the works.

The exhibition was opened by the Mayor of Droitwich Spa, and the staff and academicians from Manchester Academy all arrived, as did friends and family from near and far. The whole affair was a tremendous success – even colleagues of mine in Birmingham came. Her old neighbours from Cheshire came too, and also her new neighbours and members of the art club here in Droitwich. I've merely touched the surface of the occasion.

Mum had even been advising and gently teaching the granddaughter of one of her neighbours, who I believe went on to study art as a career choice.

At this time, few of the family were aware of her encroaching health problems. Nieces and nephews came from London when they could. Ali, the youngest daughter of my elder sister, made an amazing number of visits – before we had much by way of motorways around here – just, as she would say, "to talk to Granny". Mum was a very, very wise woman, warm and encouraging to all of us – and an excellent advisor in a crisis. We all miss her, and I'm so very sorry that she didn't live to see my own progress – not only with writing, but also with my textile course, for which the design demands were met so easily and enjoyably – I'm sure because of her influence throughout my life. Not only that, but the art tradition had passed down from her side of the family for several generations from John Thompson Campbell, and is still coming to life through her grandson – and my nephew – Piers Ottey.

CHAPTER XXVIII

TRAVELLING WITH MY MOTHER

George Thomas Robert Campbell (Uncle George) – Mum's youngest brother – on leaving the navy at the end of the Second World War had made his first home in Canada, where he built a beautiful stone house for his first wife and ultimately their daughter (my cousin) in the province of Quebec, where over the years he had built up a very, very large beef station. The whole estate (one of the biggest in the province) was called, not surprisingly, Dockendale Farm – after the name of his birthplace, Dockendale Hall in Whickham, County Durham. Although he later established a major company involving shipping, which had its main offices in Tokyo, and a conference centre in Nassau, in the Bahamas, the farm, not far from Montreal, was his first love.

Having guarded British shipping crossing the Atlantic through most of the war years, he was happy to visit Canada as often as possible as he gradually recovered from his naval duties.

I spent quite a few breaks there – I loved the open country and animals all around me. Ultimately, as so much of his business time was spent between Nassau, Canada, Tokyo and Greece, I usually hosted guests (his partners) when a conference was to be held in a special building on the farm. It was very formal and overlooked the enormous hangar-like machinery storage space. It was very luxurious, and, similarly, so was his lovely residence in Nassau, which was also used for meetings as well as breaks for close family.

In the summer of 1984 my mother came with Marie and me, totally unaware of our immediate futures. It was the first time we had visited there together, though my parents had been many years earlier. George, wanting family on the beef station, had assured me of a good job as deputy manager of the current business there. I could already drive a tractor, but never before had I driven one of such a size – huge – far bigger than those in the UK. I was also a fairly good handler of animals and loved the open air. We had agreed that Marie and I, eventually, would occupy another house on the estate, which had great potential for our own skills and crafts and was very near an area where maple syrup was extracted from trees. There were so many things for us to do and enjoy – including our own swimming pool and tennis courts, which were used by the staff when family were not in residence.

We even made arrangements to split the huge cellar into two parts – one part for my weaving looms and the other part for Marie, who wanted to go also, as a workshop for her tailoring skills and her work in lace and silk – ideal in an area where there were quite a lot of businessmen with families and a need for both ladieswear and christening gowns.

In Canada, the law requires a dwelling to have one-third of its total interior – from cellar floor to roof ridge – below ground. This is because of permafrost. The basement was huge, with enough space for a weaving centre, a dressmaking and lacework centre, enormous freezers for meat, etc., and of course the inevitable tank (septic).

An interesting point regarding the residence permit: one must attend lessons in French (free) as the majority of the population has French as its first language.

Another necessity was to make sure one's view from inside the dwelling must be of at least fifty metres clear – to guard against intruders and deer, etc. While my mother painted the area one day, Marie and I went around the space round the house, marking yellow crosses on any trees less than fifty metres away. Some laws are very strict! I still have some yellow paint on an old jacket from that exercise.

My mother and father had visited there around 1973, so she was already familiar with the area. She painted most days, after I'd put together an awning made from stout posts with an old tablecloth draped over, as it was very hot in the open. A borrowed sledgehammer did the job. Great fun! The corn was high and the sky was a strong blue, but we knew that come winter it would be altogether a different story!

The river running through the estate froze – hard – but beneath the ice it still ran, forcing the ice blocks aside and even over the low walls of the tennis courts. People had to use tractors as a means of getting to work.

At Easter time we were late being picked up from Montreal Airport as all the workmen had had to clear huge blocks of ice – with tractors and other equipment – which were preventing the householders from leaving their houses and reaching the road!

I had the use of a car so we could visit many other places. At Montreal in winter all shopping and most movement is in the City Underground – a fantastic experience. One day we visited Ottawa, the capital city, and its wonderful parliament building, in the grounds of which I saw my first black squirrel! Never a dull moment!

Vancouver also is an eye-opener, and in all the areas we visited there were experiences we hoped to repeat.

Uncle George had left instructions for the farm 'boss', Claude, to teach me not only to fish (I did bring in our next breakfast one evening), but also to shoot! He put a target up in the middle of the river facing the direction of the flow, rather than across the flow, as I might well have shot one of the cows, which roamed freely in the summer. That was a great fun activity, and quite legal on one's own property!

I shall never forget a journey a long way from the farm which we took in autumn. Uncle George was with us, and he wanted to show me other areas. He was driving, and on the way back, very tired out and sitting in the back of the car for once, each time I opened my eyes it seemed as if we were racing through an inferno, if not a forest fire. It was all an illusion created by our speeding through miles and miles of forests – all decked out in their autumn finery! The colours of a Canadian fall have to be seen to be believed. A most beautiful picture!

One day in Canada we travelled upriver on a regular boat route, intending to arrive in Quebec city for some shopping. Imagine this – approaching the dock, above which the walls rose steeply (with steps, of course). We could see the huge hotel in the square up there. It was built, as were many others, when the Trans-Canadian Railway was so daringly constructed.

The sun was a blaze of setting glory as it slowly descended behind the hotel. Two young cyclists crossed the square to reach a bench, against which they propped their cycles. Out of their respective backpacks, one drew a violin and the other an oboe. Magic was in the air. I think these few words say it all. This was one of the wonderful memories I've kept and thought about – usually at sunset!

My short visit to Canada on retiring in 1986 proved to be a visit to cancel all the arrangements we had, at that point, made regarding the house we would have occupied. My mother, who had moved down to Droitwich in 1980, had a lovely bungalow not far away, but she had been ailing for some time and . . . a call from one of my nephews – Helen's son, John – alerted me to the fact that I should go home. We changed our plans, flew home, hired a car at Heathrow and drove directly to the hospital where Mum was. We saw her and made arrangements to bring her home, as she wished. I then had two years of looking after her with the help of night nurses, but sadly she died in March 1988. We'd lost Dad in 1976, and she'd had eight years on her own in Cheshire before moving to be near me. My older sister, Anne Pauline, died in 1991 and Helen in 1992, so it was an exceptionally bad few years for me. However, by then my uncle had had to appoint someone else to the post I would have filled in Canada.

Out of a job, what should I do? I had already become interested in weaving, so back to college I went, to study textiles. I was well set up at home – looms, etc. – and the work involved so many interests I already had that I thoroughly enjoyed the three years leading up to the exam. I visited my fellow weavers after college, and through the generosity of one of them, and her husband, we moved our textile activity to their house, where there was a large area we could work in and our tutor, who lived in Gloucester, could come and help us to carry on.

CHAPTER XXIX

STARTING TO WRITE AGAIN

It all started with Gwenda, really. One winter, when we had a severe snowfall, and I – an ardent snow lover – was confined to crutches following a hip operation (the second), I looked from my bedroom window to enjoy the snowy landscape – yes, enjoy it! Having a collection of bears – all characters, rather than merely teddies – I picked up Snowy, a polar bear, and posed him looking longingly out of the window. His activities formed (in my mind) the first of the words and pictures I would later turn into a book for small children.

When I showed the first verse and its accompanying photo to a Hungarian friend, she persuaded me to go on. She even volunteered a translation, so that young Hungarian children could learn English in a fun way.

> Izzy and her bears were so bored one wintry day
> They thought they'd take the camera
> And go outside to play. . . .

Round about that time, I had met, in the local supermarket, an elderly lady – we kept bumping trolleys! Finally, at the checkout, we met again. Her daughter was waiting to drive her home, but we exchanged phone numbers and a few weeks later they came for lunch.

Gwenda wanted to see what I was doing, so I showed her the first few lines and photo, which were the start of my book-to-be!

She was thrilled to bits. Having a large number of grandchildren who loved to be read to, she knew it would appeal. She looked forward to doing so if it ever got printed. It did, and she was happy to actually verbally advertise the work to others. I did, after many snags, go through with it (including a court case), and her young family members and mine, and also ex-students now with young children all eagerly received copies in due course. Just recently I've been wondering about a reprint of *Much Travelled Bear Stories*. It might happen yet!

I visited Gwenda when I could, and by that time she had carers on a regular basis. She loved me to read to her, first the stories of Paul Gallico, amongst others, then I introduced her to Longfellow's 'Story of Hiawatha' – much loved by the children I met in my final teaching practice in 1953.

Gwenda would lie back, feet up, eyes half closed, and then look at me to reassure me, "I'm not asleep, Sybil. I'm just seeing those wonderful words in pictures." I can hear her gentle voice as I write.

One day, Gwenda asked me if I ever wrote just for myself – thoughts perhaps, memories or hopes. I had sort of scribbled as a teenager, and she persuaded me to go ahead, after I produced and showed her some of my earlier efforts.

She was so sweet and insisted on giving me a helping hand towards what I now refer to as the Little Green Book. It was, again, a private production, but through the goodwill of the well-established publishers was extremely well appreciated by friends, family and old students as gifts. Recently I was so happy to receive word from three friends, all going through (to me) unbelievably hard times, that the copy I sent each of them apparently gave them a big lift.

I had attended one or two of Gwenda's big birthdays over the years, and had met many of her very large family, and I was very sad when she died (by then she was in a good nursing home) at the wonderful age of 102. I owe her a lot. Thank you to a very dear friend.

CHAPTER XXX

THE BAHAMAS

My parents were due to visit Nassau, where Uncle George had a business centre. Sadly, although prepared for the trip, Dad became so ill that he had to go into hospital.

After he died, Marie and I persuaded Mum that it would be a good time for the three of us to visit Nassau. Reluctantly Mum agreed.

Unexpectedly we had to stay one night in the United States. I forget the name of the town where we landed, but apparently our visas, unknown to us, did not allow for a stopover before our flight to Nassau. We were escorted by somewhat intimidating police to our overnight accommodation.

As one other person was 'non grata' he was taken with us! Dreadful rooms – locked doors and a police guard in the corridor all night! No breakfast in the morning but a waiting minibus to get us three to the plane. A couple from George's office were there to greet us, and they were horrified by the way we'd been treated!

Once in Nassau, in a beautiful apartment on the third floor with a large, safe balcony all around, we finally settled in tremendous comfort and – yes – luxury! Corrine – a fantastic Anglophile – came every morning to do household shopping (if needed), see to the laundry (needed every day in that climate) and generally look after us. The views! We had our own swimming pool as well as the sea, which was in fantastic shades of turquoise and emerald – I'd never seen such colour before! Trees along the water's edge were bent nearly double, forming the most crazy shapes.

We had breakfast on the terrace. There was a shop/bar not far up the road, under coconut trees, and a lovely park to visit. I also had a car to venture further afield. There were plants in profusion and fantastic colours. We were invited out and we also swam and roamed. Although we missed Dad, it was what Mum needed just then!

The town of Nassau was an absolutely enchanting place and very pro-British. Indeed, if you arrived by boat, your first view was of Queen Victoria's monument on the quayside – a reminder of past history.

The straw market was an interesting place to browse in, and when we took Mum to the Botanical Gardens seals leapt for fish from a diving board and flamingos 'strutted their best' among the flowers. Music came on the air, and those magnificent regal birds seemed to perform a prepared and gracious choreography around where my mother sat. Quite a unique experience!

CHAPTER XXXI

SNOW

Watching Sky and Eurosport, during the World Cup skiing competitions in spring, I remembered Marie and I taking her father to the very centre I was seeing on the television – Solda Sölden, an Austrian ski centre. The holiday came flashing back – while I skied they walked and photographed the area. However, it was very icy and Marie fell and broke her wrist. Rejoining them, we took her to the local clinic, where the double fracture was set and supported. Fortunately, she recovered well and was checked over on our return. In the meantime I skied for the few remaining days before leaving the ski centre.

It's been the snowy times of my life that I can remember most clearly, and it was, I think, 1982 when I was taking three and a half hours on my daily journey to Yardley – often wading waist-high through the drift, across the road to the school gate. One morning, I was horrified to see the damage to the school where the beautiful stained-glass window high up in the library was broken in places and bedecked with enormous icicles hanging over it. That window was an important part of the building's history. The water in the water tank in the roof space had frozen and then burst through. Such a shame – such a lovely piece of art!

The A38 and M5 caused a few problems, but one tended to disregard them and take care to avoid the worst of the drifts. The snow in the fields on each side rather resembled waves of the sea, encroaching on the road in places the snowploughs had yet to clear.

At that time, one weekend I took the train (at night) up to

Inverness to be met by friends who had moved from Droitwich to Nairn. David met me and took me to their lovely hillside home for breakfast.

They had, by then, most of the roads up there cleared, and they took me to many, many places of true natural beauty. On the frozen banks of one tarn we picnicked and watched the water's edge gradually freezing – like magic. On the way back to Nairn David asked me to listen to a guitar piece he had just written to see if I would write some words to the tune. Having seen the barren area of the Battle of Culloden, I did write them and they were actually printed for me in my small green book called *Thoughts Along the Way* – actually printed by the same publishers as I hope will be printing this book!

Phoning from Nairn to check that my mother was OK, and asking her what she was busy doing, I got the reply "I'm painting my winter garden from the lounge!"

My reply was a bit cheeky, so I won't repeat it here! The picture I have in my dining room is a statement in itself, and I look at it constantly.

I remind the reader of the impression I was under during some of these driving experiences – it seemed, looking to left and right, as though an angry ocean was approaching and even encroaching on the roads, so high and wide were the 'waves' of the windblown snow.

CHAPTER XXXII

FRED YEUNG

One weekend Selpar organised a day school for Polish folk dance, to which members from elsewhere would come. The University of Birmingham offered the facilities to us free if we allowed students to attend with no charge – a very generous gesture. The tutor was Tony Latham, whose mother had been one of the founders of the SIFD years ago and who was also responsible for enabling me to start our West Midlands group (Selpar).

Tony was an expert teacher, and during the course of one dance I found I was dancing with an excellent dancer of Oriental origin. He told me the route of contacts he had followed to find me, with recommendations from eminent dancers, before arriving in Birmingham.

"I don't even yet know your name," said I.

"Oh, Yeung – call me Fred!"

It was the start of a good friendship! He was truly gifted, and I asked him if he was busy on Tuesday evenings.

"Reading, thinking, etc., etc.," he replied.

"How about joining us?" I asked him.

"Yes!"

And from then on he was a regular in class, in performance and in energy! He was with us until the end of the summer term, when his fiancée, Helen, came to join him so that they could then travel home to Hong Kong for their wedding. Thank you, Fred. It was great to have you – both – for the time you had with us.

Unbeknown to me, he had asked Helen to get a certain gift for him to give me when he left! It's a beautiful gold bird on the wing, and it is very precious to me. Thank you, Fred and Helen – sincerely.

Sometime later, a letter arrived from Hong Kong, requesting a week of my time to teach Hungarian folk dance to various established ballet schools and folk-dance clubs. Arrangements were all in place for what was the most interesting booking I'd ever had – flights, accommodation and a professional fee all in the one package! What a chance that was, both as a teacher and as a traveller!

Alas, disaster befell me when, through my doctor, I received a date for my hip-replacement surgery. The possibility had been creeping up on me, and with my usual casual approach it had gone completely out of my mind! I was absolutely mortified that I could not accept the invitation. I have, over time, been invited frequently to visit SIFD groups in the UK to pass on some of my hard-earned Hungarian expertise, frequently having to travel to other groups almost as soon as I was home from Hungary. However, having been so active for so many years with activities involving 'impact' it should have come as no surprise. But it was the biggest disappointment I have ever had to face.

For the Hong Kong groups and classes, help was at hand and my ex-student Leslie Haddon was able to fill the gap. These things happen, I know, but it's still a big blow when they happen to you!

Some months ago, when at least twice daily we saw Hong Kong in combat during a period of great student unrest, not unnaturally I was concerned for the two young people I had to come to know so well. As it happens, they were OK, I think. They wrote to me to tell me that, having taken all legal preventative actions with regard to the coronavirus, they had to come to the UK to look after their younger son, whose boarding school prohibited all Asian students from going home, and also their elder son, who, having achieved a degree at Cambridge University, was embarking on a course at Oxford University to gain his Masters degree.

In Fred's letter he told me they were both very anxious to see me and were keeping a Saturday free so that they could come and visit me. They would then return to Oxford, pick up their two sons and return to Hong Kong.

They arrived at my house and plied me with gifts. They were so happy to meet up again. When we went to our local pub for lunch, I made sure I was wearing my Hungarian jacket plus bird brooch – it's absolutely right for it, and the occasion!

I was able to give them a gift of a table mat from my loom, a girl's everyday blouse, skirt and apron, known as *kék festo* (it's in blue-and-white printed cloth), and a pair of boots to go with it. For Fred I had a rather superb embroidered man's shirt which I had brought back from a trip sometime to Budapest.

Later I had a lovely letter and photos of the three of us at my front door. We look so happy.

*Selpar (SIFD), performing outside Birmingham Town Hall,
Chamberlain Square, c.1986.*

*Selpar in Droitwich shopping centre before going on a 'Dance Safari'
in the Cotswolds.*

Selpar at a dance festival.

*Selpar – West Midlands group – SIFD, minutes before a performance.
Costumes representing the colours of Israel.*

CHAPTER XXXIII

MY KITCHEN WALL

When the house was newly built, the kitchen walls were plastered, and then we found an attractive paper for the main wall. The dining room lies on the other side of this wall.

Ultimately tiring of the paper we'd used, I stripped it off. Now blank, I took advantage of its plainness and, laughing at the possibility of the timber I intended to use being removed by a future owner, I took a stick of charcoal and sketched out my two favourite childhood 'friends': Winnie the Pooh and Mickey Mouse, who are still there, behind the timber!

My kitchen wall! The original spur to my writing.

Remembering the skills Ted Kestle had taught me, I measured it up very carefully, bearing in mind the need to keep two areas near floor level clear for the plugs I'd need when using electric appliances during cooking, etc. From our local hardware and building-material shop in Droitwich – Bullocks – I purchased thirty pine floorboards with tongue-and-groove edges, ninety-six by four and a half inches.

First I had to prepare the wall and the adjacent protruding side of an inset storage cupboard (under the stairs). Strips of pine (one and a half by half an inch) were fixed horizontally to the now comically adorned wall and the small wall at right angles to it. For this, I drilled and plugged then screwed the strips to the wall. The vertical pine panels were comparatively simple to position – though very stiff shoulders resulted. As each one was lifted to the next, pins were hammered home to fix them in place.

With the use of a plumbline I checked that the walls were absolutely vertical, and on the bit at right angles I found there was a slight lean away on both sides. So, measuring carefully, I marked the two affected planks to square them up when fitted.

I needed help – with my small saw I couldn't cut the line up the whole plank length accurately enough for the fit needed, so I returned to the supplier and asked his help!

I can still hear him saying, "Those lines ain't plumb, love!"

My reply: "You ain't seen the corner of the wall I'm fitting."

When all was assembled, I'm glad – and proud to say – it was a perfect fit.

Later came the shelf at just above table level and brackets to fit for support. I was so happy with the ultimate result! Thank you, Ted – a teacher worthy of the title! Boxing in the two areas of electricity sockets, with mitred corners, I finished the whole thing with what a carpenter would call 'quarter round' – an edging which sealed the tops of the pine to the ceiling and round the two sockets – and it was finished. Job completed, the planks all having been treated to three coats of boat varnish, between sandings. Still, today, it looks quite new. If necessary, the whole wall can now, if I wish, be wiped down with a damp cloth.

Over the years, many gifts have been added to the wall, each one reminding me of someone or somewhere. One of these gifts was given to me by an elderly lady who ran a B & B where I stayed by Lake Balaton, after I pruned her roses before leaving her!

Needless to say, the two (birthday of 1968) gifts were the first to hang there, on the wall. Other gifts followed – each with its own tale to tell.

CHAPTER XXXIV

FORTUNES OF WAR

Thinking back all those years to when we were a family in a country very much at war, I realise how fortunate we were not to lose any of our relatives, but we were able slowly and gradually to return to our normal routines. My mother's family included three brothers, each one involved in either the army, air force or Royal Navy; but none of my father's seven sisters suffered the loss of a husband, despite all of them, I think, being involved in warfare. His two brothers, one of whom was in the RAF, also survived.

One day in particular from this time will live with me forever and remind me of so many families who suffered in the infamous Holocaust.

I was just twelve years old when an old school friend of my father's – Flying Officer Bill Young – called to see us on his way back to his base. It was 1945/6, I think. He was a photographer and with his team he had been involved in the opening-up of the horrendous camp at Bergen-Belsen. He had called to show my father the photos taken by himself and his team at that time.

When the two men left the dining room for a brief few minutes, I crept into the room to see what was going on! My horror knew no bounds when I saw the photos laid out on the table. No, I should not have been there, but when 'Uncle Bill' went back to tidy up and collect the evidence he realised that I, the youngest of the three of us, had seen the horrors!

Years later, in Budapest with my friend Anthea, we joined

a group of tourists to undertake a full tour of what, I think, is the largest synagogue in Europe – and surely it is the most beautiful. It was a most enlightening experience and added greatly to my knowledge of the war years and the aftermath thereof. We were shown a photographic display, including most of the concentration-camp photos I'd seen as a child. I was utterly horrified to be informed that after the war many Jewish survivors, some of who had since emigrated, had been able to return to their homeland, and on seeing the photos many had actually recognised themselves at the time of their release!

We saw the beautiful museum where treasures that had been so well and bravely hidden were displayed and preserved for posterity.

In the garden of the synagogue we saw the most wonderful and beautiful Tree of Remembrance – a large weeping willow. To this day I remember its long pointed leaves sparkling in the sunshine. Each tiny silver (metal) leaflet had a name engraved on it, and together they danced in the slight breeze. I took a photo of the tree to give to Eva, a member of the Selpar dance group. As she was of a Dutch family who had all survived the events in her homeland it was much appreciated.

At this moment in time, we can look back and forward, thankful that so many brave people survived to tell the tale.

During the war I always knew that one of my uncles was on leave when I arrived home from school and saw a cap and Sam Browne belt on the hall table!

One of my uncles, Athol Lester Campbell, was largely instrumental in getting most of his men back from Dunkirk. Then after a short leave he was sent off to Africa, where Rommel and his Italian soldiers were fighting in the desert. Athol Campbell was highly decorated more than once.

Many years later, on a visit to Canada with my mother to show her what I hoped to do a year or so later, we took her to see Uncle Lester at a residential home for ageing army personnel (as we also have here)! By now he was a full resident and, as with all ex-officers, had a good, kind batman to help him. My Auntie Grace joined us there also. His attendants had pushed his chair near the entrance gates of the home; and when we saw him wave, Mum walked slowly towards him.

Even after a stroke he recognised his loving sister and called, with many a crack in his voice, which I can, even in retrospect, hear, "Na-a-an-cy!"

He repeated her name quite a few times, and we all had tears of happiness as she sat gently with him. His beloved sister was so relieved to see him. We left them together for a while, and I'm so glad they had that time together as he died after another stroke a few weeks later.

ACKNOWLEDGEMENTS

Amongst all the wonderful people I have known, or read about, two stand out particularly as being the reason for my writing this autobiography, or even attempting it: Mary Walshe and Noel Fitzpatrick.

Miss Mary Margaret Walshe, the headmistress of both my first two schools, was skilled in dealing with a very gradual change in the far-reaching organisational system of education. She acted with common sense in all situations and was instrumental in opening new doors for 'new' teachers. I am grateful for the encouragement she gave me in that situation, and I was influenced by the way she accepted new ideas from those she helped along in their careers.

The autobiography of Professor Noel Fitzpatrick is written with conviction, revealing his constant care, as a vet, of both animals and their human owners. He punches straight from the shoulder, and tells it as it is! Thanks to him, that is what I've tried to do!

And of course my mother and father ensured a good education for me, leading me forward along the way. The way they themselves surmounted problems, particularly during the war, was an example to me. The art I inherited from my mother was influential in giving me success when I gained a distinction in advanced City and Guilds textiles – sadly, just after her death. I'm still convinced she knows.

I am also grateful to friends I know and have known and all the boys and girls I've met along the way, including those who, in some sad cases, I've helped (I hope) in return.

Magda Osskó (Osskó Endréné) opened up a whole new vista for me – and my pupils at school! Her patience and trust in the work to which she opened my eyes (and feet) knew no bounds, and through her love for her country and all its traditions she assured me of success and imparted to me a great affection for Hungary, which I still feel and will always feel.

I must also acknowledge the pleasure I had working with and for the wonderful teachers and members of our SIFD groups from Edinburgh to London and all those places in between.

Mrs Eileen Carradine, whom I met at Yardley Grammar School, helped me in my work there and has continued to do so by reminding me of many of the changes we went through. She sent me information regarding some of those changes – and challenges. Eileen is a friend to cherish. She encouraged me, taking an interest in my writing of both the book of bear travels, *Much Travelled Bear Stories*, and my somewhat introspective collection entitled *Thoughts Along the Way*.

Big questions: will there ever be an opportunity to meet again all those wonderful girls and boys through whose diligence I gained my promotions? Will I ever return to the country of my heart? Will I ever again sing '*Himnusz*'?

Anthea Hollingshead has supported me all these years through ups and downs, many involving hospitals and surgical procedures. She has done for me, by taking responsibility for my disorganised way of dealing with paperwork, what I promised her mother I would do for her – I said I'd be there for her, as she has been for me. Bless you.

I must also give thanks to my neighbours, June and Alan Colyer, for so much help with regard to medical emergencies (June) and plumbing or electrical problems (Alan). A good team indeed! I would have been in great difficulties had they not been there for me.

A fairly frequent phone call was "June have you got a minute?" This was *always* answered with "I'm on my way."

Kelly, a young mother of two lovely lads, came to me as part of an Age UK system of 'reconnection' – visiting and helping those who live mostly alone. She has welcomed the chance to help with some of the initial typing of this saga. I am also grateful to her mother, Sharon, who joins us sometimes.

Mrs Di Kemsley is not only a good friend, but as my Girl Friday she is of inestimable help, particularly just now. She has been coming to me each Friday for many years as my home help, and without her my energy would be sadly overtaxed and my house very much the poorer. Without her great housekeeping skills I would be in a great muddle, and she has also been a great encourager in this latest writing venture of mine.

I must add my thanks to Arthur H. Stockwell Ltd, publishers, for their patience and kindness, and for coping so adventurously with my problems in publishing this book.

My first book, *Thoughts Along the Way* (also published by Arthur H. Stockwell Ltd), helped not only me, but also many of my friends, and now some of my fellow patients in hospitals. I hope all those who have supported me in this venture have enjoyed my trials and tribulations. I know they have been numerous, and everyone's efforts must, at times, have been very frustrating – but here it is at last – with my heartfelt thanks to you all.

My first test on a lathe, fruit bowl and table lighter.